ANGLICAN VISION

Emmanuel Amand de Mendieta

LONDON

S·P·C·K

1971

First published 1971
by the S.P.C.K.
Holy Trinity Church
Marylebone Road
London NW1 4DU

Printed in Great Britain by
The Talbot Press (S.P.C.K.)
Saffron Walden, Essex

© Emmanuel Amand de Mendieta, 1971

This book has been published with the help of a grant from the Trustees of the Bethune-Baker Fund.

ACKNOWLEDGEMENTS

Thanks are due to the following for permission to quote from copyright sources:

Cambridge University Press: New English Bible second edition © 1970 (with Oxford University Press)

Geoffrey Chapman Ltd: *Documents of Vatican II* (1967), edited by Walter J. Abbott, s.j.

Harvard University Press: *English Modernism* (1927), by H. D. A. Major

Longmans Green & Co.: *Early Christian Creeds* (1950), by J. N. D. Kelly; *Essays in Christian Politics* (1927), by William Temple

The Book of Common Prayer 1662 is Crown copyright; extracts used herein are with permission.

SBN 281 02599 1

Contents

Foreword

Some years ago Dr Amand de Mendieta published a book, *Rome and Canterbury: A Biblical and Free Catholicism* (1962). It aroused considerable discussion and, in those pre-Second Vatican Council days, even controversy and (perhaps for some) a measure of distress. After all, it was not an everyday occurrence for a Roman Catholic, a monk of the Order of St Benedict, a Belgian, and a theological scholar of international reputation, to be received into the Church of England.

That book contained a moving autobiographical account of the author's "spiritual pilgrimage" from Rome to Canterbury. In a second section, it set forth the theological grounds and implications of that pilgrimage. It was not an exercise in polemics, although the view of Rome it presented was inevitably coloured by the author's personal experience. Looking at it again now (and all readers of this new book should study the earlier one) one is again impressed by its fundamentally irenic spirit: a spirit wholly characteristic of its author's own nature. None the less (and I believe Dr Amand de Mendieta would agree) some parts of it belong very much to the era which, in Rome, was drawing to an end with the pontificate of Pope John XXIII and the far-reaching developments which were inaugurated by the Second Vatican Council.

In this new book, Dr Amand de Mendieta focuses his sights much more closely upon the Church of his adoption, and not only the Church of England but the Anglican Communion as a whole. With a typical and admirable Gallic desire for clarity and precision, he would like to see an Anglican theology and ecclesiology more unified, though not simply uniform. No doubt, Dr Amand de Mendieta now has not only a greater experience of us as well as a keener and more critical eye for our own situation and problems. As always, he is optimistic. This, apart from acute analysis, is what makes his book so refreshing. He makes us look at ourselves in new ways, from unaccustomed perspectives. Insofar as his book achieves this, it will not only aid our own growth in self-renewal but also forward the greater ecumenical cause. Perhaps the kind of synthesis of views he commends lies in a more distant future than we should like. At the very least, however, to read this book is to face oneself the problems and

questions it poses. It is all the more opportune in that the questions
he asks are not often enough the questions which we ask ourselves.
For this alone, Anglicans everywhere are in his debt.

Of course, in Anglicanism the established Church of England is
in a different situation from Anglican provinces in other parts of the
world. As Dr Amand de Mendieta well knows, this is part of the
historical legacy which the Provinces of Canterbury and York cannot
simply wish away. (Any more, say, than the Roman Catholic community in the United Kingdom can loose itself from its own history
in relationship to Anglicanism as a world-wide communion.) There
are features of the author's analysis which apply well enough in
England but which, in varying degrees, would not seem so important
in, say, the United States, New Zealand, Africa, or maybe even Wales
and Scotland. One cannot pretend that local and historical matters
do not affect us. This does not mean, however, that the notion of an
"Anglican Vision" lacks relevance for any part of our Communion.
There are parts of his work with which we may (in one part of the
world or another) agree or disagree. What I believe most of us can
say is that in this book some of the pertinent questions are raised. It
is a statement, of high seriousness, which none of us can ignore.

A final and personal word. It has been my privilege to know and
to count as a friend the author for many years, when he was in Cambridge and while he has been Canon Residentiary of Winchester
Cathedral. His own home has been a kind of microcosm of ecumenism. There, informally, one could meet Christians—Roman Catholic,
Orthodox, Anglican, and Protestant—in a spirit of total acceptance
and mutual regard. This is yet another great gift which the author
has brought to his adopted Church. We would be poorer without it,
as well as without this book which sets forth the author's hopes,
prayers, and vision.

HOWARD ROOT

Preface

In 1964 I contributed a short essay "From Anglican Symbiosis to Anglican Synthesis" to the symposium *The Anglican Synthesis: Essays by Catholics and Evangelicals,* which was edited by Canon W. R. F. Browning.[1] Some of my friends have since urged me to develop this essay into a book on the subject of my vision of the future for the Anglican Communion, and on the subject of Anglican unity and diversity. They urged me in particular to put before a wider public my small contribution for promoting a more coherent and authentic unity within the Church of England, a unity conceived, of course, in the ecumenical perspective.

My first reaction to this pressure was of doubt and misgiving. I was —and still am—very conscious of the fact that I was received into the Church of England only fifteen years ago (1956), and it may seem to be presumptuous of me to urge the members of my Church to draw closer in faith, theology, and liturgy, in life and in love. I am also acutely conscious of my limitations and my ignorance, especially of parish life and of the problems of the Church's responsibility in social matters.

However in the end I put aside my fears and misgivings, and I write this book in the hope that a simple, plain and, to some extent, a personal witness will not be without value. In my earlier works I have printed full bibliographies, and inserted on every page appropriate footnotes. But, for the present purpose, I hope to express my own views in a straightforward style for non-specialists, without sophistication, subtlety, or theological jargon, even though my testimony may run the risk of seeming too subjective

Just because of my unusual position among members of the Church of England, I feel an obligation to write in all humility a plea for a stronger unity in that Church, including all forms of legitimate diversity. I fancy that I can look on her, as she is today, with a more detached outlook than those of her members who were born English and reared as Anglicans, for I am neither English by birth, nor Anglican by heredity or tradition, but I know a good deal of the three great Churches of Christendom, all founded on the Catholic Tradition. I was baptized, confirmed, and ordained priest in the Roman Catholic

Church, and I lived for more than twenty years as a Benedictine monk. I feel a deep veneration and love for the Orthodox Church, especially the Greek and Russian Churches. I was received into the Church of England in June 1956, and I have since ministered in this Church as a priest; since October 1962, I have held the office of a Canon Residentiary of Winchester Cathedral. I trust therefore that it is not presumptuous to claim that I am at a centre or focal point of a triangle formed by the three Churches, and that my observation of the Church of England is not that of a man viewing her from outer space.

I am confident that my readers will easily understand and accept the limited scope of this book. In the first chapter, I try to explain some basic notions about the purpose and meaning of Christian unity, and to outline the Catholic idea of a visible, corporate, and sacramental reunion of the divided Churches.

Then I submit a short historical evaluation of the Anglican Reformation of the sixteenth century and of the Catholic Movement in the Church of England. I assume that my readers know the main facts of the Anglican Reformation, and I shall therefore confine myself to sketching a tentative assessment of this important episode in the history of the English Church.

In the third chapter I describe briefly the present Anglican theological spectrum and the main traditions or schools of thought in the present Anglican Church. I intend also to show that the contemporary Church of England, considered as a sociological phenomenon, is gradually growing from the state of friendly co-existence between the different traditions or tendencies, to a state of a more coherent and practical unity.

Then, in the following chapters, I discuss my particular theme, my vision of the future for the Anglican Communion, laying great emphasis on the necessity of a strong unity perfectly compatible with a very large diversity, not only in the present Church of England, but also—and mainly—in the great Ecumenical and Catholic Church of the future.

I hope that I may be able to convey to my readers my own vision of the place of the Church of England in the plan of the divine Providence for the establishment of the great and reunited Catholic Church of the future. I see her ideal destiny as one of the most powerful forces in the reunification of the now divided Churches into the great Coming Catholic Church of the twenty-first century.

At the end of this personal preface, it is my pleasant duty to express my heartfelt gratitude to all the friends who helped me by their spoken or written advice to improve this work, to stimulate me by their critical observations, and to correct my inaccuracies and errors.

Among those who helped me by their constructive criticisms and suggestions I should mention, in the first place, the Reverend Canon W. R. F. Browning, of Christ Church, Oxford, who read carefully all the manuscript and proposed many *addenda, delenda,* and *corrigenda.* Also I must express my gratitude to Mrs Anita Pheby, to the Reverend Piers Nash-Williams, and especially to Mr Michael R. Bruce, who took the trouble to read and correct all the first draft of this book. I cannot forget five theologians who represent the different schools of thought within the Church of England, and who so kindly clarified for me their various positions. They are: the Reverend A. H. Simmons, the Reverend F. P. Coleman, the Reverend Dr J. I. Packer, the Right Reverend C. W. J. Bowles, bishop of Derby, and Professor W. H. C. Frend.

I must also mention with gratefulness my dear wife Ginette, who spent an enormous amount of time typing and typing again the constant revisions of this book. She alone knows the extent of the debt of gratitude I owe to her permanent collaboration and penetrating criticism.

I cannot express enough my sincere gratitude to Mrs Margaret Duggan, who twice read the typescript and suggested many necessary improvements and corrections. If this book is drawn up in correct English, all the merit is hers. She carried out for me and with me, for the benefit of the readers, an enormous and competent task of abbreviation and correction.

EMMANUEL AMAND DE MENDIETA

Winchester, 1971

1

The Meaning of Christian Unity

This book is written on the assumption that it would be highly desirable for almost all the extant Churches and denominations—only excluding certain distorted Protestant sects—to join in a visible and organic unity, and that the Anglican Communion, of which the Church of England forms a part, has something precious and unique to contribute to this unity. In my essay "From Anglican Symbiosis to Anglican Synthesis", I tried to give a provisional answer to the question: What is the nature of the contribution which the Anglican Communion can make to this desirable transformation into the Catholic Church of the future, and in what way does the Anglican house need itself to be set in order, to find a higher and deeper internal unity, and so to make this contribution possible and effectual?

Since that essay was written primarily for theologians accustomed to the use of a special terminology, I wrote largely in philosophical and theological language, but I hope that the present work will be read by a wider public of intelligent men and women interested in church matters, though not necessarily trained theologians. So, in the first instance, I must ask and answer two fundamental questions.

1. Is there in fact any useful purpose to be served by achieving a visible and organic unity and union between the existing Churches and denominations? If so, what is its purpose?

2. What exactly is meant by the term "Christian Unity"?

1. THE PURPOSE OF CHRISTIAN UNITY

All of us know that it was the expressed wish and the prayer of the Lord Jesus that all those who should put their faith in him as their Lord and Saviour should be perfectly one. At the end of the farewell discourses in St John's Gospel, we read these moving words:

But it is not for these alone [the apostles and disciples] that I pray, but for those also who through their words put their faith in me; may they all be one: as thou, Father, art in me and I in thee, so also may they be

4

in us, that the world may believe that thou didst send me. The glory which thou gavest me I have given to them, that they may be one, as we are one; I in them and thou in me, may they be perfectly one. Then the world will learn that thou didst send me, that thou didst love them as thou didst me. (John 17. 20-3, N.E.B.)

For convinced Christians the passage from Christ's solemn prayer for his Apostles and his Church, just before his redeeming passion, is sufficient evidence of his fervent desire for the perfect unity of all his disciples in the centuries to come. However, there are many today, especially young people, who desire to be committed Christians, and yet cannot accept so authoritarian a statement: without being sceptical, they are nonetheless critical. It is not therefore enough to say that this priestly prayer of our Lord Jesus is our main motive for seeking a perfect and organic unity with those Churches and denominations which are now divided. We must also show, if we can, what were his reasons when he prayed so earnestly for the perfect and organic unity of all his followers for all time. Perfect unity in faith, love, and life should indeed prevail among all true believers during their earthly pilgrimage to the Eternal City, for that unity is an image and a reflection of the perfect and indissoluble unity of nature and love which exists between the Father and the Son in the glorious Trinity: "As thou, Father, art in me, and I in thee, so also may they be in us". Among men, this perfect unity must be organic.

Pragmatic arguments appeal to Anglo-Saxons; these critics would appreciate an empirical demonstration that the mission of the Church, now divided into Churches, would be furthered by their reintegration into one visible, organic Church. Moreover it is important to stress that the great reunited Church, able to speak with mightier authority and with one voice, would command more respect and carry more conviction on all vital matters of faith, morality, society, and religion. Yet I am persuaded that there is something even more important, namely that, in the great Ecumenical Church of the future, her members (clergy and laity alike) would regain many of those *charismata*, or special gifts of the Holy Spirit which were a peculiar feature of the early Church. It is beyond question that all divisions and schisms between existing Churches have in the past considerably interfered, and still interfere, with the loving and unifying work of the Holy Spirit.

2. THE MEANING OF CHRISTIAN UNITY

Both within and outside the Church of England, people are increasingly accustomed to pray, and to hear prayers, "for the unity of all

Christian people", but they seem to have a very different idea about the meaning of the term Christian Unity.

Some seem to think that they are seeking a single, monolithic, and uniform church structure, world-wide in scope, within which all professed Christians would worship according to identical rites and ceremonies and would be subjected to one authoritarian, universal, and uniform jurisdiction, discipline, organization, and hierarchy. In spite of the present crisis of authority and faith in the Roman Catholic Church, many people erroneously believe that this Church is now, and will continue to be, a mainly juridical, massive, homogeneous, and monolithic Church. They shy away, very understandably, from this false conception of her as a tyrannical organization, and they say that they reject Christian unity in this form. Indeed it is a caricature of the true Christian unity and union.

Others think of unity as nothing more than a confederation of Churches, and they fail to see that denominationalism must "die", even that the *present* Church of England must "die", if this true unity is to be achieved. Such people are apt to be Protestant-minded, and to consider the sacraments as optional extras. They are satisfied with such platitudes as: "We are already all brothers in Christ", or "The actual divisions between Christian Churches and denominations are not so serious as many people claim. Let us have an effective confederation of the existing Churches and denominations; that is enough for all practical purposes".

This loose federalism coupled with an eventual "inter-communion", and a real, organic, and permanent unity in faith and sacraments, are two different things indeed. These two forms of church unity show a close analogy with the two stages of the organic reunion of the Church of England and the Methodist Church, as they were proposed in the final Scheme *Anglican-Methodist Unity* (1968). In this final Report of the Anglican-Methodist Unity Commission, we can see precisely how the idea of confederation of Churches alone, or the idea of entering into full communion with another Church, but keeping the Churches separate and distinct (the so-called intercommunion), is an inadequate substitute for a real organic, sacramental, fully integrated unity and union. Confederation or intercommunion may be a necessary stage on the road to perfect Christian unity, which cannot be attained till this first and indispensable condition has been fulfilled, but intercommunion is not in itself sufficient: it is only a means to the end of organic union.

On the contrary, a single, uniform, authoritarian, and highly centralized Church or Super-Church would be too vast, too massive, too crushing, too inadequate for the different national and cultural needs, and too unwieldy.

Nevertheless to have two or more Churches existing side by side, in full mutual communion, *in the same place or area* (as was provided for the first stage of Anglican-Methodist unity in the last Report of 1968), would be, at best, wasteful of resources and effort and a very provisional expedient in order to reach an organic and complete union. At worst, the loose confederation of Churches, vaguely united by intercommunion, may be an open invitation to that kind of disunity and party spirit which the Apostle Paul so sternly condemns (see 1 Corinthians 1. 10-13).

Plainly the Ecumenical Movement is spreading everywhere, even in the Orthodox Churches, even in the Roman Catholic Church. Its basic aim should be the visible restoration throughout Christendom of the faith and order of the undivided Church, as they existed during the first ten centuries of our era.

By this I do not imply a material or identical restoration of the Church of the first millenium, but I plead for a *dynamic* restoration of the one, holy, catholic, and apostolic Church. In the new formulations of the Catholic faith and of the essential theological truths, in the developments of the diverse theological speculations and theories, in the diverse liturgical adaptations to the diverse languages and civilizations, in the new adapted and relevant social and evangelistic activities, this dynamic restoration would include all the advances, acquisitions, and attainments of mankind, since the Great Schism between East and West, all the spiritual, intellectual, moral, scientific, and technological developments of our human race.

This basic aim of the Ecumenical Movement is thus not merely the establishment of a mutual sentiment of charity and better understanding between the separated Christian bodies of our time, or the creation of new organizations for friendly co-operation and better relations between them. Such collaboration, as we see in the beneficial activities of the World Council of Churches, may have—and has indeed—very good results, but it is only a necessary preliminary stage to something deeper. Let us suppose that one organization including all the separated Churches can be established in the form of a general confederation of the Churches. Even then, this imaginary federal Super-Church would be still very remote from the "One Church, one faith, one Lord" of the New Testament. Just because this confederation of Churches could be established to deal with the problems of life and work, it would easily become a positive hindrance to a real organic reintegration of Christianity, just because many people would fall into the error of mistaking it for the reality of the full organic reunion in faith, sacraments, and order.

We must stress the danger of any allegedly "Ecumenical Project" to band the various non-Roman Catholic Churches together in some kind of Pan-Protestant confederation, with or without the Orthodox Churches. The venerable Roman Catholic Church is the largest of all the separated Christian Churches; any scheme for the reunion of Christendom which, in theory or practice, excludes her, can only produce a travesty of reunion. No one can ignore the fact that the Second Vatican Council promulgated, on 21 November 1964, the extremely important and open-minded Decree on Ecumenism, *Unitatis Redintegratio,* which begins with these words: "Reunion among all Christians is a cause which the Second Vatican Ecumenical Council has set itself to promote as one of its principal aims".

Having tried to say what Christian unity is not, I shall try to put into words what is, or rather what will be, this complete and organic unity for which we so often pray. If asked, all thoughtful and Catholic-minded members of any Church would say that perfect unity and reunion will come in God's good time, when he wills and by the means he wills, and that it will be embodied in the great Catholic Church of the future, postulated and demanded by our faith. The essential characteristics of this unique supra-national Church will include perfect unity and communion in the Catholic faith, perfect unity and communion in sacraments and order, and perfect unity and collaboration in love and in mutual fellowship. I do not mean, of course, any outward and stereotyped uniformity in theological opinions and speculations, or in the outward forms of worship, devotion and Christian life. In the words of the old maxim, I mean: "In necessary things unity, in doubtful or unnecessary things freedom, in all things love and charity".

When the Lambeth Conference met in 1920, it delivered, in its Appeal to all Christian people,[2] a noble message of great historical importance on which much subsequent ecumenical work has been based. It gave the world a vision of what organic Christian unity could and should be. Much has happened and much has been written since 1920. In particular, the Roman Catholic Church is now officially and wholeheartedly taking her place in the world-wide Ecumenical Movement. This inspiring Appeal continues, however, to be one of the most decisive statements of Anglican hopes for unity and of the way to achieve it.

I shall quote some passages of this brave and moving document which was a landmark in the history of church reunion.

After acknowledging "all those who believe in our Lord Jesus Christ and have been baptized into the name of the Holy Trinity, as sharing with us membership in the universal Church of Christ, which is his Body",[3] the bishops clearly defined what they understood by the term "the Catholic Church".

> We believe [they wrote] that God wills fellowship. By God's own act, this fellowship was made in and through Jesus Christ, and its life is in his Spirit. We believe that it is God's purpose to manifest this fellowship, so far as this world is concerned, in an outward, visible, and united society, holding one faith, having its own recognized officers, using God-given means of grace, and inspiring all its members to the world-wide service of the Kingdom of God. This is what we mean by the Catholic Church.[4]

Then they went on to describe the unhappy divisions of the Church, and the great Churches which stand outside the Anglican Communion and are separated from it, and continued:

> We cherish the earnest hope that all these Communions, and our own, may be led by the Spirit into the unity of the Faith and of the knowledge of the Son of God. But in fact we are all organized in different groups, each one keeping to itself gifts that rightly belong to the whole fellowship, and tending to live its own life apart from the rest.[5]

The causes of divisions lie deep in the past and are by no means simple or wholly blameworthy. Yet none can doubt that

> self-will, ambition, and lack of charity among Christians have been principal factors in the mingled process, and that these, together with blindness to the sin of disunion, are still mainly responsible for the breaches of Christendom. We acknowledge this condition of broken fellowship to be contrary to God's will, and we desire frankly to confess our share in the guilt of thus crippling the Body of Christ and hindering the activity of his Spirit.[6]

The times call us to a new outlook and new measures. The Faith cannot be adequately apprehended and the battle of the Kingdom cannot be worthily fought, while the body is divided, and is thus unable to grow up into the fullness of the life of Christ. The time has come, we believe, for all the separated groups of Christians to agree in forgetting the things that are behind, and reaching out towards the goal of a reunited Catholic Church. The removal of the barriers which have arisen between them, will be brought by a new comradeship of those whose faces are definitely set this way.

The vision which rises before us is that of a Church, genuinely Catholic, loyal to all Truth, and gathering into its fellowship all "who profess and

9

call themselves Christians", within whose visible unity all the treasures of Faith and order, bequeathed as a heritage by the past to the present, shall be possessed in common and made serviceable to the whole Body of Christ. Within this unity, Christian Communions now separated from one another would retain much that has long been distinctive in their methods of worship and service. It is through a rich diversity of life and devotion that the unity of the whole fellowship will be fulfilled.[7]

I add one more quotation:

The spiritual leadership of the Catholic Church in days to come, for which the world is manifestly waiting, depends upon the readiness with which each group is prepared to make sacrifices for the sake of a common ministry, and a common service to the world.

We place this ideal first and foremost before ourselves and our own people. We call upon them to make the effort to meet the demand of a new age with a new outlook. To all other Christian people whom our words may reach, we make the same appeal. We do not ask that any one Communion should consent to be absorbed in another. We do ask that all should unite in a new and great endeavour to recover and to manifest to the world the unity of the Body of Christ for which he prayed.[8]

It would be difficult to improve on this message, so generous and so Catholic-minded. It states very clearly that, if there is to be any visible corporate and organic union of the Christian Churches in the future, the only realistic basis for that reunion will be that which is Catholic and traditional—the Catholic faith and order, the Catholic sacraments and the ministry of the one undivided holy, catholic, and apostolic Church.

We Anglicans are fortunate in that we have inherited and maintained the traditional "order" of ecclesiastical life, with its emphasis on the sacraments and the threefold ministry of bishops, priests, and deacons. It is happily impossible for us to consider the visible and organic unity of the Church as a matter of secondary importance. Ever since the Reformation, many leaders of the Church of England have consistently asserted that the visible and future unity and reunion of the universal Church will not be reached without the general acceptance of some fundamental doctrines. This "basic minimum" of doctrine was expressed (perhaps in somewhat pragmatic terms) in the well-known "Lambeth Quadrilateral".

This four-fold statement, issued by the Lambeth Conference of 1888, is so important that I quote it in full. The basis of Christian unity is expressed in the simplest terms and with great economy of language. Because the Anglican Church or Communion is part of the catholic and apostolic Church, the statement proclaims:

A. The Holy Scriptures of the Old and New Testaments as "containing all things necessary to salvation", and as being the rule and ultimate standard of faith.

B. The Apostles' Creed, as the Baptismal Symbol; and the Nicene Creed, as the sufficient statement of the Christian faith.

C. The two sacraments ordained by Christ himself—Baptism and the Supper of the Lord—ministered with unfailing use of Christ's Words of Institution, and of the elements ordained by him.

D. The historic episcopate, locally adapted in the methods of its administration to the varying needs of the nations and peoples called of God into the unity of his Church.[9]

This "Lambeth Quadrilateral" expresses the strict basic minimum for the reunion of the Churches.

While the present schisms persist (between East and West, and inside the Western Church), the Church of England and all her sister-Churches in the Anglican Communion are bound to pray and work, with faith and in a spirit of repentance, for the final and complete restoration of the unity of the Catholic Church. As Anglicans, we believe that our present membership of the Church will never find its true and complete expression, until all committed Christians have accepted, in union with the Lord of the Church, the one Catholic faith, Eucharist, and ordained ministry.

3. THE CATHOLICITY OF CHRIST'S CHURCH

By the term "Catholic Church" we do not, of course, mean the contemporary Roman Catholic Church. She is only one particular Church or Communion in spite of her numerical superiority. In the present situation, and owing to our unhappy divisions, the Catholic Church does not subsist in all her perfection and integrity either in the Eastern Orthodox Church, or in the Roman Catholic Church, or in the Anglican Communion, or in the other Churches which issued from the Reformation. But ideally and in spite of the present divisions, the Catholic Church exists in the great historical and separated Churches, mainly to teach the truth of the Gospel in its fullness.

This true Catholic teaching finds itself in opposition to any teaching which is defective, or one-sided. A Catholic-minded man rises above the limitations of his age, temperament, class, race, culture, or country. Though he may have a natural interest in some facet or aspect of Christian truth, he does not ignore or deny other complementary aspects. On the other hand, a heretic isolates and exaggerates a

11

truth or a partial truth to such a degree that it almost becomes a false-hood, and he shuts his eyes to all other aspects of that truth.

The popular antithesis of Catholic and Protestant is too often mis-conceived. Every genuine protest against error should be based on real knowledge and sincere love of truth. This axiom applies not only to scientific argument but also to theological discussion and speculation. A real Catholic, who loves truth in this manner, must protest against any error which limits or denies the truth of the whole gospel. Every thoughtful Christian theologian (I include of course theologians of the Orthodox Church) should wish to be both Catholic *and* Protestant. They should be, at the same time, firmly rooted in the immutable Catholic or Orthodox faith, *and* protesting, with discretion and true charity, against all abuses and theological distortions, against all kinds of mutilation and watering-down of the truth.

One of the worst effects of the present divisions among the Churches and denominations is that each of them tends to emphasize its distinc-tive features against those of all the others. As we can see in particular in the innumerable Protestant denominations and sects, these new fragmentations and distortions flourish in isolation, and their votaries become more fixed and intractable in their views.

If we truly desire a genuine Christian unity, we must pray and work for a renewed Catholicity, in which all partial truths and authentic forms of Christian life will be combined in the wholeness and balance of Catholic faith, of the essential theological principles, of Catholic sacramental life, order, and devotion. This is what I call "the Catholic synthesis".

The providence of God has given to the Church of England a special responsibility and opportunity in this task of Catholic reintegra-tion. Even at the time of her protest during the Reformation, the newly-reformed Church found a place, in her official declaration of doctrine, for some important matters which had become obscured or forgotten by the medieval Western Church. She tried to integrate these in a general pattern of life and liturgy which can be called Catholic in that it was inherited from the universal Church of the past. The Church of England continues to have this difficult and necessary task of doctrinal, liturgical, and pastoral integration within her own life and structure. Her successes and failures have had, have now, and will have in future, great significance for Christians belonging to other Churches and denominations not actually in communion with her, and will make a great impact on them.

We Anglicans have set before us this ideal and goal of gradually

12

building up the full Catholicity of the great Ecumenical Church of the future—a goal to be attained by God's grace, by means of prayer and ceaseless effort. We need greater and purer missionary zeal, free from any taint of insular, nationalist, imperialist, or cultural bias; we need greater earnestness, humility, and intellectual charity in searching for, and welcoming, new or forgotten truths. Only in this way can the Church of England be truly Catholic, and become, in God's good time, a stage towards, and the model of, the great Catholic Church of the future—the goal to which the Ecumenical Movement is today feeling its way. She must not be afraid to abandon her present organization, outward appearance, individuality, and establishment privileges, for it may be the price to be paid for her advance to the fulfilment of the vision and the ideal of the great Catholic Church of the future.

2

A Survey of the Past

1. A TENTATIVE EVALUATION OF THE ANGLICAN REFORMATION OF THE SIXTEENTH CENTURY

Queen Elizabeth I, during her long reign (1558-1603), sought to establish firmly a comprehensive church settlement that would, at least in theory, embrace all her subjects. It was intended to be both Catholic and Protestant, but never papal. It was Catholic in that it was built on the foundation of the Bible as holy Scripture, on the long-held Catholic faith, and on the tradition of the early Church expressed in the first ecumenical councils and the writings of the Fathers. It was Protestant in that it rejected the supreme and universal power and jurisdiction of the Pope, the doctrine of transubstantiation, the private masses for the dead, indulgences, lay communion in one kind, compulsory clerical celibacy, compulsory auricular confession, and the medieval doctrines of purgatory and merit.

This Elizabethan Settlement of the national or State Church of England cannot be called glorious. It was not so much a pacification of the contending forces as a practical compromise between them, in which the Queen tried to bring all the existing religious parties and all the persons of very diverse views into the national Church. The motive for such a compromise was, above all, political: the Queen and her advisers looked on the national Church as a department of the State in which uniformity of practice was an essential condition of stability. Therefore some of the doctrinal formulae which were drawn up as part of this settlement were deliberately worded in comprehensive—even in ambiguous—terms. In their mention of certain theological points, the compilers of the Thirty-nine Articles at times succeeded in saying two things simultaneously with extraordinary adroitness. But the settlement was never meant to conciliate the definitely Roman Catholic or Recusant party or to bring it into the national Church. What was required was to provide a *modus vivendi* between those who supported episcopal government and Catholic theological principles, and the Protestant-minded Puritans who had returned from exile abroad wedded to Calvinistic theological principles and to the Genevan methods of church polity. The government had to find some basis of agreement on which both parties could work together in a state of peaceful co-existence as agents of the State, regardless of the theological differences between them.

Though this settlement is hardly glorious, this gradual consolidation of an independent and national Anglican Church must be included among the achievements of the Elizabethan period. The Christian Church in England was neither created, nor re-created, by Elizabeth's Acts of Supremacy and Uniformity, and even at the time of her death forty years later, nobody could discern the Church's full potentiality and destiny. By that time Richard Hooker, in his *Laws of Ecclesiastical Polity* (1594-7), had gone a long way towards a definition, very skilfully presented, of an ideal Anglicanism; but the English Elizabethan Church had not reached that balance between Catholic and Protestant doctrines and practices which Hooker hoped to see. Up to that time, the Elizabethan Church had been in spiritual matters not merely Protestant or Calvinistic, but, to a remarkable degree, Puritan.

The Reformation in England and the Reformation on the Continent which started with Luther and Calvin, developed on somewhat different lines. The English Reformation was affected by English insularity, by English political and social forces, and (especially in the reigns of Henry VIII and Edward VI) by the crying needs of the royal treasury. It may have been government-sponsored, but it developed into the gradual "Protestantization" of the English people, and in time there grew up a special English brand of Protestantism. The State was not always in favour of this process, but the effect was to influence directly and indirectly the development not only of English life, but also that of the whole of Western civilization.

In this section, I shall try, with much diffidence, to draw up a balance-sheet of the Anglican Reformation of the sixteenth century, taking into account mainly those matters which formed part of the Elizabethan Settlement.

I. THE CREDIT SIDE

(1) *The maintenance of the Catholic Faith*   The main positive principles on which the Reformation was ostensibly based were the free and gratuitous divine gift of grace and salvation in Christ, the absolute sovereignty of God's grace and of the gospel over every institution

including the Church, justification granted by grace alone in Christ and apprehended by faith alone, the sovereign and supreme authority of the Scriptures, and the emphasis on a personal and theocentric or Christocentric religion. All these principles are in perfect agreement with the Catholic faith, and are indeed necessary to its fullness.

In so far as the Reformation was a protest, it was a protest, sometimes violently expressed, not against the Catholic faith or the Catholic Church as such, but against an accumulation of abuses in church discipline, against serious doctrinal omissions or distortions, against the excessive Roman juridicism and Western institutionalism, and, above all, against the unhealthy development of the doctrine of the papacy, and of the papal supreme jurisdiction and administration. It was a protest against certain attempts within the medieval Western Church to lessen or attenuate, if not to deny, certain crucial doctrines which were always essential to the well-being and integrity of the Catholic faith, and proclaimed as such by the Fathers, both of the East and the West.

This is the context in which we have to consider the historic decisions of Archbishop Cranmer, of Archbishop Parker, and of Queen Elizabeth, as to how far they would accept, and impose on the national Church, the prophetic Reformation protest against the papal abuses, and, at the same time, retain the new Reformation movement within the traditional English framework of the Catholic faith and institutions. To many British or non-British Protestants and to many Roman Catholics, this historic decision has always appeared strange and paradoxical, but it is not so. The first great Anglican Reformers, such as Archbishop Cranmer, Bishops Latimer and Ridley, and even the more fanatical Hooper, wished to see a powerful renewal and purification of the *Ecclesia Anglicana*. They hoped for a far-reaching reformation of the medieval English Church, but always on the foundation of the pure Catholic faith of the gospel and of the tradition of the early Church. None of these Protestants, all of whom died at the stake, wished to introduce a new theological system of their own devising, such as Calvin's masterly, but one-sided, theological systematization. Their successors, such as Parker, were working in more favourable circumstances internally and internationally, which made the Elizabethan Settlement possible. None the less, the fact that this attempt could be made, and was in fact made with such firmness, in Elizabeth's reign, may be regarded as one of the most important of all the developments in religion or in politics which took place in the sixteenth century. Both in England and elsewhere, it was a period of turmoil, characterized by violent nationalism, under the leadership of absolute monarchs, which was combined with a vivid, though often fanatical, Christian faith.

The most important achievement of the English Reformation and, in particular, of the Elizabethan Settlement, is indeed the survival and maintenance of the Catholic faith in its essentials. Here I use the word "faith" as distinct from "theology". No essential part of "the deposit of faith" was rejected or sacrificed. The so-called "protest" of the Reformers was peacefully inserted into the traditional structure of the Catholic faith, as it is expressed, for instance, in the so-called Apostles' Creed and in the Nicene Creed, namely the Symbol of faith of Nicaea-Constantinople, and was made more explicit. This insertion into the Thirty-nine Articles was easily made, because the great dogmatic principles of the Reformers, in their positive content, are indeed integral parts of the full and pure Catholic faith. Let me give just one example: the strong emphasis on the sovereignty of God's grace and of the gospel over the Christian "religion" and over the institutional structure of the Church, is not a peculiar feature of the "Protestant faith", but a very important article of the Catholic faith as expressed in the writings of all the Fathers, particularly in the treatises and biblical commentaries of St Augustine of Hippo who was so much admired and quoted by Luther, Cranmer, and Calvin.

(2) *Catholic and Biblical Liturgy: The English Bible* The second great item on the credit side of this balance-sheet is that, on the whole, the Anglican Reformation maintained the essentials of the Catholic liturgy of the Western Church, which was translated into English so that the people could understand it. Undoubtedly there were many deliberate and regrettable omissions, and some insertions of controversial words and sentences which could carry a heretical meaning if they were to be construed in an exclusive sense.

The Anglican rite of Holy Communion was based on the old Roman rite in the form followed in England according to the "Use of Sarum": the eucharistic service in the first English Prayer Book of 1549 is a free rendering in English of the Sarum Missal. Much of the old order, with considerable omissions in matters of detail, was retained and skilfully adapted so as to avoid some of the later developments of medieval eucharistic doctrines (such as on eucharistic sacrifice and transubstantiation), and to emphasize the memorial and symbolic aspects of eucharistic theology in which the Reformers were particularly interested. The Holy Communion service of 1549 shows indeed a greater continuity with the old Roman Mass than any important English eucharistic service now in use in the Anglican Communion. It is marked by some measure of the sobriety and restraint of the pure Roman rite of the first seven centuries, before the admixture of later elements.

Under the influence of the advanced or Zwinglian reforming party, the 1549 Communion service was drastically revised, and this service in the Second Edwardine Prayer Book of 1552 was much more "reformed". Even if Cranmer did not personally compile this second Prayer Book, he must have approved of it. It has made an enduring impression on the English rite and has given it a distinctive character, marked by its own Protestant and one-sided eucharistic theology. The 1552 revision was followed by those of 1559 (under Elizabeth) and of 1662 (under Charles II), which both show some modest attempt to establish a kind of *via media,* and to restore the balance in a more Catholic direction.

But, to be fair, one of the most beneficial results of the Reformation in general, and of the English Reformation in particular, was to put the Bible, translated into the national language, in the hands of all the faithful, so that they might come to know and love it. Not only was the Bible translated into a rhythmical and majestic style, and put, wide open, into the hands of all English Christians, and on the lecterns of all the churches, but also the use of the Bible in the English language made the liturgy once more collective and communal.

(3) *The maintenance of the episcopate*   Another outstanding feature of the English Reformation was the maintenance of the historic and Catholic episcopate, and the preservation of episcopal order and jurisdiction. On several occasions there were sweeping changes of personnel among the bishops, yet the episcopal succession was never visibly broken. It was preserved throughout the reign of Edward VI, even when the Zwinglian party almost succeeded in imposing their brand of extreme Protestantism on the English Church after her separation from Rome. It was preserved by Queen Elizabeth, who realized that without the historic episcopate, the necessary uniformity of religious practice could not be maintained, and that the national Church would break up into sects, fall into anarchy, and become the victim of civil strife. Even when the bishops were convinced and militant Puritans, it was the episcopate which linked the Church to her past and ensured order and discipline in Church and State. Elizabeth may not have taken the highest view of the episcopal institution; practical and political considerations were probably the most powerful motive for her

action in filling at the start of her reign the sees which were vacant because of the death or deprivation of Marian bishops. Even so, special care was taken to ensure that the new bishops then appointed were validly and ritually consecrated, so as to ensure the historic continuity of the episcopal office.

The Elizabethan bishops were united by loyalty to the Queen and her church Settlement, and also by a common resistance to the recusant Roman Catholics and to the extreme Calvinistic Puritans, both of whom refused to accept that Settlement. Most of the bishops themselves were moderate Puritans who did not believe that the episcopate was necessarily either apostolic or the best form of church government, but they did maintain that the English government of Church and State might lawfully organize the Church with an episcopate, and that, in that event, neither the action of the government nor its acceptance by themselves, was contrary to the authority of the Scriptures. Supporting the shrewd moderation of the Queen and of Parker, the Elizabethan bishops were eager to show that past abuse does not inevitably forbid present use, and that it was a false principle to assert that the national Church of England was bound to discard all the practices of papal rule.

It was not until the end of Elizabeth's reign that some divines and bishops began to stress the importance of the apostolic succession of the bishops. According to this doctrine, the Bishops are indeed the holders of a ministry founded by Christ, demanded by Scripture and apostolic practice, endued with divine authority, and transmitted by the Church through the centuries. Influenced by the eirenical teaching of Richard Hooker, these bishops and theologians were the forerunners of the so-called Caroline Divines, those Anglican theologians of the seventeenth century who developed what are commonly called "High Church" principles.

Another consequence of the preservation of the episcopal order and jurisdiction was the maintenance of the belief in the mission of the Church as the accredited guardian and administrator of the sacraments and the other appointed means of divine grace. This belief was upheld on a double level, that of the Catholic or universal Church, and that of the national Church of England. As a religious and social fact, the maintenance of the episcopacy had the inevitable result of restoring self-confidence to the Church, even at times when she was dominated by Puritan bishops and distressed with internal conflicts and tensions. In the beginning, Zwinglian and then Calvinistic Protestantism had great influence in the English Church, but this lessened throughout the Queen's reign and only the extreme Puritan zealots found that their cherished doctrines were incompatible with the episcopacy, even when most of the bishops themselves were Puritans. In the person of the primate John Whitgift (1583-1604), who waged war against extreme Puritans on behalf of law and order, these extremists met an Archbishop who was as vehemently opposed to their ideas as any Pope, and who had the backing of all the resources of the civil power.

We must recognize that the historic conception of the Church as both divine and human, universal and national, held its own, and steadily grew in strength, in spite of the dangers to her spirituality which were involved in the political conditions of Elizabeth's Settlement. John Jewel, bishop of Salisbury (died 1571), Richard Hooker, and many other divines who wrote during the last decade of Elizabeth's reign, were utterly loyal to the Reformation, and recognized the Protestant and protesting attitude of their Church vis-à-vis the contemporary Church of Rome. Nevertheless, they proved that such loyalty was consistent with a theology and with forms of worship hallowed by antiquity, and they justified the *via media* of the Church of England as scriptural, primitive, and truly Catholic. The position of a national Church, taken up and defended by Archbishops Parker and Whitgift, was to be defined more clearly in the next century by Archbishop Laud and his followers.

The gradual shift in the theological concept of the Church, a consequence of the acceptance of Hooker's great work, marks the undermining of the Puritan dominance and the recovery of the *via media* tradition which avoided the rigours of orthodox Calvinism, deprecated Puritan bibliolatry, stressed the role of reason in the interpretation of the Christian faith, and resisted the extreme Puritan demands for Calvinistic changes in liturgy, in church government, and in the Thirty-nine Articles. This more Catholic movement was not simply based on the new liberal tendencies manifested in continental Protestant theology. It can be regarded as a restatement of the Anglican *via media*, foreshadowed two generations before by the moderate Anglicans of the reigns of Henry VIII and Edward VI, and always to be detected in the pages of the Second Prayer Book of 1552, and of the less controversial Elizabethan version of 1559.

II. THE DEBIT SIDE

(1) *The royal supremacy over the national Church* The Reformation in England was an act of the Sovereign, or rather of the State as

embodied in the Sovereign and Parliament. Henry VIII, Edward VI's government, and Elizabeth aimed at the foundation and establishment of a national State Church, the actual Church of England. At the same time they desired this national Church to keep a dogmatic, theological, and liturgical continuity with the English Church and the whole Western Church of the Middle Ages, though without the Pope, "the foreign Bishop of Rome".

By the first Act of Supremacy (1534), Henry VIII became, in fact and in law, the Supreme Head of the national Church, and the King-in-parliament gave a sanction to the Church's revised organization, to her doctrinal formularies, to her public worship, and even to some extent, to her doctrine. The Privy Council and royal ministers took cognizance of ecclesiastical affairs. The sovereign co-operated with the bishops and convocations in the government of the national Church, and appointed bishops and commissions to determine appeals in ecclesiastical affairs. All this followed from Henry VIII's break with Rome, and was fixed and established by the legal settlement in Elizabeth's reign.

Let us look more closely at the break between the Church of England and the "Bishop of Rome", and at the Act of Supremacy of 1534 by which Henry and his successors were granted the title and function of "the only Supreme Head in earth of the Church of England". These two facts can only be understood in the context of contemporary England, with its ardent and unanimous support for the Tudor monarchy and its sudden outburst of nationalism and insular pride.

With such an anticlerical and xenophobic climate of opinion, no sovereign or his advisers could be much interested in the international and supranational character of the Catholic Church. In practice, Henry and his successors were dealing exclusively with a national Church which they considered to be an obedient, subordinate, and useful instrument of national unity and national policy.

It would be inaccurate to try to ascribe the repudiation of the papal power and jurisdiction only to the strongly nationalist feelings of Henry VIII and his Parliament and to their desire to rid themselves of papal fiscal exactions. It is clear from the historical facts that Henry VIII and, thirty years later, his daughter Elizabeth were both determined to be fully and absolutely masters of their kingdom, and to suppress any exercise therein of any "usurped and foreign power and authority, spiritual and temporal". Henry VIII, Edward VI, and Elizabeth all bluntly refused to be subject in any degree to any foreign spiritual jurisdiction of the Pope. With the utmost force, they asserted their determination to hold themselves the chief ecclesiastical and civil power in their realm. Considering themselves as "godly princes", truly appointed by God himself, they believed themselves entitled to exercise their royal functions as supreme Rulers and Governors both of the State and of the national Church.

The Henrician theory of royal supremacy over the national Church, which I think to be erroneous from the Christian and Catholic point of view, is formally stated in the preamble of the Act of Restraint of Appeals, which was passed by Parliament, not without much opposition, in February 1533. The King, now called the Supreme Head of the Church of England, possessed the plenary and entire power, authority and jurisdiction in all causes, matters and debates, "whether they be ecclesiastical or civil".[1]

This theory of royal supremacy over both the Church and the State of England is again solemnly defined in Article 37 of the Thirty-nine Articles.

The King's Majesty hath the chief power in this Realm of England and other his Dominions, unto whom the chief Government of all Estates of his Realm, whether be Ecclesiastical or Civil, in all causes both appertain, and is not, nor ought to be, subject to any foreign jurisdiction.

Where we attribute to the King's Majesty the chief government, by which Titles we understand the minds of some slanderous folks to be offended; we give not to our Princes the ministering either of God's Word, or of the Sacraments, the which thing the Injunctions also lately set forth by Elizabeth our Queen do most plainly testify; but that only prerogative, which we see to have been given always to all godly Princes in Holy Scriptures by God Himself; that is, that they should rule all estates and degrees committed to their charge by God, whether they be Ecclesiastical or Temporal, and restrain with the civil sword the stubborn and evil doers.

The Bishop of *Rome* hath no jurisdiction in this Realm of England."

The Henrician break with the papacy and the unhappy separation of England from the Roman Catholic Church were probably in the historical circumstances inevitable, and a divine judgement pronounced over the Roman Catholic Church, as also over the Church of England. We must indeed take into account the stubborn refusal of the popes and the Roman Curia in about 1530 to deal radically with the blatant abuses, and to institute the reforms demanded and carried out by Luther and afterwards by Calvin.

But the result of this schism was for England the real danger of Erastianism. All the Tudor rulers were convinced that, as "godly princes", as Supreme Heads or Governors, it was their bounden duty strictly to control the national and subordinate Church, and to legislate for her in almost every matter. In the person of Thomas Cranmer we see a perfect example of an Erastian theologian and bishop. We may surmise that all Elizabeth's bishops were in fact Erastian, because Erastianism was presumed by the Elizabethan Settlement.

(2) *The ruthless changes in public worship*   The traditional liturgy in Latin of the medieval Church, with all its venerable associations, was suddenly and ruthlessly suppressed and banned as popish and super-stitious; in its place the forms of the Prayer Books of 1552 and 1559 were imposed by the Sovereign and Parliament. Even if these did not entirely obliterate the old familiar forms and rites of the Latin Mass and the other liturgical ceremonies, they partially obscured them, and the new service of Communion was often celebrated with a Calvinistic bare-ness of ritual and simplicity of vestments. It was indeed a strange contrast with the solemnity and gorgeous ceremonial of the pre-Reformation rite that was familiar even in the parish churches.

In Edward VI's reign there was a general destruction of stone altars which were replaced by wooden communion tables (1550-1), and also the violent confiscation, during the regime of the Protector Northumberland, of church plate, eucharistic vestments, and Latin service-books. All the valuables were to be handed over to the royal commissioners. They had to hand back what was necessary for the revised forms of divine service to the incumbent (two chalices might be retained for cathedrals and large churches!) and to leave a sufficient stock of surplices. They had to deliver the rest of the goods to the master of the Jewel House (1553). If ready money was found, it also could be taken, and was to be handed to the treasurer of the Mint. This confiscation was still in progress when Queen Mary came to the throne. The seizure of chantries and the confiscation of liturgical plate, missals, and vestments, marred the public image of the Reformation in the eyes of many people.

Because of the violent emotions, hatreds, and prejudices of the time, and to meet the pressing financial needs of the King and the greed of many royal servants, the Anglican Reformation went much further in a revolutionary and destructive direction than was either necessary or required by these principles of moderation and of the "middle way" between Rome and Geneva which Cranmer and Parker professed. Its drastic purging of medieval rites, traditions, and practices not only eliminated everything that was clearly corrupt and harmful or of doubtful value, but also many other things which were, in their own way, valuable and worthy of preservation.

(3) *The suppression of the monasteries* A spectacular example of wholesale destruction was the complete and indiscriminate suppression of all the monasteries of men and women in Henry VIII's reign through the good offices of Thomas Cromwell. Dom David Knowles, the outstanding authority on the history of religious orders in England,[2] is convinced that there were a number of religious houses of high reputation where monks and nuns still led a strict and holy life. The only explanation for the action the King took against these monasteries was his anxiety to replenish his treasury which, as always, was empty.[3]

On the other hand, there was a larger number of other houses (priories and cells of monks and nuns with less than ten inmates, and almost all the houses of the Augustinian Canons) of which the continued existence served no good purpose whatever, and which seemed incapable either of reforming themselves or being reformed; these deserved to be dissolved.[4]

But between these two sizeable groups, there was a considerable number of medium-sized and large houses which were sufficiently harmless and respectable to be allowed to continue. They needed a purge and a tonic, some drastic reform administered by the royal or the ecclesiastical authority; but instead of this, the voracious King preferred to dissolve them all, great and small, making no distinction between them and treating them all as a means of refilling his treasury.

Yet we must not be unfair to Henry or to Thomas Cromwell. Apologists of the monks, who have described "a reign of terror" and "the cruel tyranny of Cromwell", have misunderstood the situation, or have transferred to the England of 1536-40 the mentality of reformers and revolutionaries of other lands and of other times. As a matter of fact, this great undertaking of the suppression of all the monasteries was carried out with the minimum of personal violence. Nevertheless it affected intimately the lives of thousands of educated English men and women of the time, transferred a considerable proportion of the national wealth from the possession of the religious orders and congregations to that of the King, brought about the plundering and demolition of many churches, and eliminated from the English scene a traditional way of Christian life.

The dissolution of the monasteries involved considerable losses in matters of art. Many precious manuscripts were lost in the dispersion of the monastic libraries; many church furnishings and ornaments, such as altars, chalices, and other vessels, vestments, missals, retables, candlesticks, thuribles, organs, pulpits, and pictures were sold to the speculators or dealers; many perished by destruction and decay. We can but guess the extent of the loss of the beautiful monastic buildings from what still remains either in ruins or in partial use. Another artistic loss was the sudden end of the splendid gothic style as a living form of architecture.

(4) *The loss of some ancient occasional services, and the abolition of the eucharistic vestments*   Another important spiritual loss in the liturgical field was the complete suppression, by the Second Prayer Book of 1552 and the Elizabethan Prayer Book of 1559, of the very popular and pious ceremonies for the feast of the Purification of the Blessed Virgin Mary (the blessing of the candles and the Candlemas procession), and for Ash Wednesday (the blessing and the imposition of ashes). In these "reformed" books hardly anything was left of the solemn and moving Holy Week services of the ancient and medieval Latin Church. The only services prescribed by these books for Palm Sunday, Maundy Thursday, Good Friday, and Holy Saturday were the normal services of Mattins, Holy Communion or Ante-communion, and Evensong. All the old beautiful and dramatic services, which the Roman Missal or the Sarum Missal had included, were swept away by Cranmer to satisfy the prejudices of the Reformers.

Another negative feature of Anglican Reformation was the abolition, by the 1552 Book, of the eucharistic vestments. The more traditional 1549 Book had directed the priest to wear, during the celebration of the Eucharist, "a white alb plain, with a vestment or cope". In the West the traditional vestments of a priest when celebrating Mass or Eucharist were the amice, the alb, the girdle, the maniple, the stole, and the chasuble. After 1559 the wearing of a surplice at Holy Communion was compulsory, and, throughout Elizabeth's reign, the Puritan party was strongly opposed to this practice. Their refusal to comply was for them a matter of real importance, because they detected in the surplice a connection with popery. This obligation continued to be a source of bitterness and of polemical literature, especially from the extreme Puritan party.

For over two centuries the traditional priestly vestments fell into almost complete disuse in the Church of England, until they were revived in some churches about the year 1850, and violent controversy over their use raged for the rest of the nineteenth century.

(5) *The Puritan character of the Elizabethan Church*   It would be unfair and ungenerous to place the very marked Puritan character of the Elizabethan Church entirely and unreservedly on the debit side of

the Anglican Reformation balance-sheet, but I am not an Englishman, and I cannot pretend to like either Puritan austerity or Calvinistic theology. The Puritan predominance in the Church of England during the Elizabethan era was, on the whole, damaging to that Church, by reason of the supremacy of its one-sided Calvinistic theological outlook, its contemptuous rejection of the Catholic past, and by the extreme (and at times hypocritical) severity of some of its adherents.

In 1588 some extreme Puritan tracts, violent and often scurrilous, appeared under the pseudonym of Martin Marprelate attacking episcopacy. But neither Calvin nor Knox condemned the episcopal office, while Hooker supported it without any trace of fanaticism, and only denied the absolute necessity of episcopal ordination. Except for Matthew Parker, all the notable earlier Elizabethan bishops had been in exile during Mary's reign and had strong links with Geneva, Zürich, and Strasbourg. In addition Cambridge University was dominated and pervaded by Genevan spirit and Calvinistic theology, which inspired the minds of the young men who were to go out to the parishes of England. The real growth of the Protestant spirit among the English clergy springs from this steady flow of Puritan recruits to the ministry, whether moderate or extreme, and not from Elizabeth's first episcopal appointments in 1559 or from subsequent resignations and deprivations.[5]

The sober, moderate Puritan tradition continued strongly in the Anglican Church during the seventeenth century, and we can detect many of its features even in those churchmen who are entitled, by reason of their theological principles, to be called High Churchmen and Arminians. This tradition pervaded the whole Church of England and even at the height of Laud's career, she never began to look like a Church of the Counter-Reformation. It is still a gross misuse of language to call the Laudian party "Anglican", while refusing that label to their Puritan opponents or to their Puritan predecessors.[6]

In its extreme form the Puritan religion was opposed to any kind of traditionalism in the Church; therefore it held that any kind of monasticism was, at the least, irrelevant and useless. It tended to reduce all worldly, political, and economic questions to moral problems; aesthetic and intellectual values were subordinated to moral goodness. Though it taught strict sobriety and moderation in all matters, it did not concentrate its attention exclusively on sexual morality. The deliberate mortification of the flesh, too reminiscent of popish superstition, was usually taken by Puritan writers to be the outcome and even the source of spiritual pride. The basis of moral life, and also of religious belief, was to be sought in the Bible, which the Elizabethan Puritans exalted not merely above the Church in general, but above all Protestant churches of their time. Yet they were not guilty of fundamentalism in the sense of attaching equal authority to all parts of the Bible, and the extent of their over-emphasis of the Old Testament has been frequently exaggerated.[7]

Without any doubt the most authoritative statement of the Puritan theology of the Elizabethan era is the Thirty-nine Articles of Religion which were published by Convocation in 1571 in their final form. They are certainly not entirely and rigidly Calvinistic, but they formulate as the official theological doctrine of the national Church, a mild, comprehensive, and mitigated form of Calvinism: this is particularily evident in Articles 13, 17, and 18. Though there is little in them to offend directly adherents to Calvinistic theology, these Articles (at once Anglican and Puritan) express the classical doctrines of the Reformed Protestants in flexible formulae, stating, for instance, that men are justified by faith alone, that the grace of the sacraments is received only by men of faith, and that the Church can teach nothing which Scripture does not contain.

In spite of their high and severe standard of biblical morality, we cannot help criticizing the extremists among the Elizabethan Puritans for their excessive contempt for the medieval and Catholic past, for their insensitivity to sacramental values, for their inordinate concern with the Calvinistic doctrine of predestination, with their supposed assurance of personal salvation, and for their fussy rejection of external signs as modest as the surplice, the marriage-ring and the sign of the cross in Baptism. Also, like Luther, they were prone to admire the Apostle Paul of the Letter to the Romans almost to the exclusion of a christological theology based on the four Gospels.[8]

2. THE CATHOLIC REVIVAL OF THE NINETEENTH AND TWENTIETH CENTURIES

The Catholic Revival in the Church of England, which started with the Oxford or Tractarian Movement, may be considered as the counterpart to the Anglican Reformation of the sixteenth century, and to the Evangelical Movement of the eighteenth century. Certainly a survey of the Catholic Revival would be necessary to complete the picture of the history of the Church of England, because the Catholic tradition is important in the Church of England as an ecclesiastical tendency or school of thought and as a notable factor in her historical

3

evolution. This Catholic or "High Church" tradition, which is complementary to the Protestant or Puritan tradition, stresses the historical continuity of the "reformed" Church of England with Catholic Christianity, and so upholds a Catholic conception of the authority of the Church, of the claims of the episcopate, and of the nature of the sacraments.

We can detect traces of this school of thought or "party" even in the Elizabethan age, when such men as Richard Bancroft and Richard Hooker resisted the attacks of the Puritan Reformers, but it was only in the seventeenth century that its leaders became known as "High Churchmen". The Catholic tradition was then maintained by such men as Lancelot Andrewes, William Laud, Anthony Sparrow, Herbert Thorndike, Thomas Ken, and many others, who are often known collectively as "the Caroline Divines". The party was much weakened after the deposition of James II when the clergy were required to take the oath of allegiance to William and Mary. Many High Churchmen, eminent for piety and learning, refused to take this oath and went into schism as "Non-Jurors". Those who remained in the Established Church were excluded from ecclesiastical preferment as being tainted with Jacobitism and, for the most part, fell into obscurity. But the High Church tradition continued throughout the eighteenth century and into the nineteenth century, when *Tracts for the Times* (1833-45) received an enthusiastic reception from High Churchmen of the older generation.

It was the Oxford Movement which reasserted the importance of the High Church tradition in the Church of England, though it only succeeded after a very bitter struggle.

I. THE THEOLOGY OF THE CHURCH AND THE SACRAMENTS

It is generally accepted that the Oxford Movement sprang from John Keble's Assize Sermon (14 July 1833), and that it placed a new emphasis on the Catholic and apostolic character of the established Church of England and on the order of episcopacy. Its chief objects were the defence of the national Church as a part or "branch" of the divinely instituted Catholic Church, the defence of the doctrine of the apostolic succession, and the defence of the Book of Common Prayer considered as a rule of faith.

These aims were publicly proclaimed in the famous *Tracts for the Times* begun by Newman in 1833. The Movement, whose acknowledged leaders were Keble, Newman, and Pusey, gained many influential supporters but was soon under attack by the liberal party in

Oxford University, and by the bishops. Within the Movement itself there gradually arose a party which tended more and more towards submission to Rome. Newman himself, after his famous *Tract 90,* was condemned by most of the bishops in 1841 and retired to Littlemore; on 9 October 1845 he was received into the Roman Catholic Church.

The Oxford Movement placed, and (more generally) the Catholic Revival, has continued to place a strong emphasis on the Catholic conception of the Church universal. This emphasis on the supranational Church has been substituted for the Reformation emphasis on the Church of England as a national Church established by law. The Church universal or Catholic is conceived as a living organism, ideally co-extensive with the world, as a body of which Jesus Christ is the head, and as a dwelling-place of the Holy Spirit, by whom she is governed and sanctified. The Church exists not only to proclaim the gospel message, but also to carry on the priestly work of Christ, to administer the sacraments, to remit or retain sins, and to dispense the Lord's manifold gifts of grace. The priest, in celebrating the Eucharist or in absolving a penitent, and the bishop, in ordaining and confirming, act not on their own behalf or on behalf of some group of Christians, but as the instruments and representatives of the whole Catholic Church. The priest or bishop stands in the continuous stream of the historic and apostolic ministry of the Church.

Throughout its history the Catholic Movement has fought vigorously to establish and maintain the independence of the national Church in spiritual matters and has been opposed to the ingrained Reformation tradition and practice of English Erastianism, which claims for Caesar (in modern terms, for the State) that which must be rendered only unto God. All the leaders of the Oxford Movement during the Tractarian period, and their successors in the succeeding ritualist period, fought bravely for the spiritual independence of the English Church, not only against the Crown (including Queen Victoria personally), the government, parliament, and the press, but also against their own bishops, most of whom were at that time either rigid Evangelicals or subservient to the State. Between 1833 and 1850 the bishops, the majority of whom were chosen by the government from submissive "Establishmentarians", showed themselves very hostile to the Catholic Movement, preferring to keep the national Church in complete subjection to the civil power, deprived of her rightful independence, and even of the capacity to speak for herself. In 1852 the combined pressure of the Evangelical Movement and of the growing Oxford Movement proved sufficient to force new life into the

Convocation of Canterbury, which met for the first time after more than a century of servile silence. The Convocation of York followed the example of Canterbury in 1861.

The Catholic Revival contributed enormously to the development of a sacramentalist theology according to the Catholic dogma, especially in matters of eucharistic theology. The leaders of the revival vigorously affirmed once more the real presence of Christ in or under the consecrated elements, and the sacrificial character of this sacrament, in accordance with Catholic dogmatic tradition and the teaching of the Caroline Divines.

Another feature of the sacramental life which they revived, was the restoration of sacramental and auricular confession before a priest, a practice fiercely opposed by a majority of the bishops who deplored habitual confession as un-English and urged the dangers of this practice. Over a long period, the theologians of the Catholic Movement had to struggle against a mass of ingrained prejudices and to show that the penitential practices of the Anglican Church fully recognize the beneficial nature of this sacrament as a divinely appointed method of forgiveness of sins.

II. THE DEEPENING OF THE SPIRITUAL LIFE

This is not the place to emphasize one of the most outstanding results of the Catholic Movement, the development and deepening of the spiritual life in the Church.[9] I will content myself with recalling the humble, quiet, and saintly figure of John Keble (1792-1866), vicar of Hursley in the diocese of Winchester.

The son of a scholarly Anglican priest, John Keble learned from his father the strong sacramental religion which marked his whole pastoral life. It enabled him to develop a deep and serene faith, with its devotion to the Eucharist and to the Blessed Virgin Mary, and an emphasis on sacramental confession. He looked for guidance to the teaching of the primitive and undivided Church and to the Fathers rather than to the Reformers, a feature which distinguished him and his friends from the contemporary Evangelical school. It was through this Catholic piety and theology that his spirituality developed, pure and untroubled, free from the restlessness of John Henry Newman and Richard Hurrell Froude.

The development and deepening of the spiritual life in the Church of England can be demonstrated by one obvious test: the celebration of the Eucharist in the contemporary Church. In the vast majority of parishes throughout the country, the Eucharist is now celebrated at least once a week, reverently and with some seemly ceremonial, even if the additional externals be no more than stole and altar lights. In many parishes, the Eucharist—and no longer Mattins—now constitutes the principal act of communal worship either with congregational singing or as a solemn celebration with full ceremonial.

III. THE REVIVAL OF MONASTIC AND RELIGIOUS LIFE

The English Reformers, following the Continental example, abolished monasticism, one of the reasons being their hope of raising the general spiritual level of Tudor England to which the Reformation was granted, or on which it was imposed. But their experiment in suppressing all organized forms of monastic and religious life in England, had precisely the opposite effect, just because it provided no definite scope and institutional pattern for that complete self-consecration to which, in all ages of the Church's history, many men and women have felt themselves called. Moreover, if the Church was to reproduce fully in this world, even if only in some groups or communities, the heroic, celibate, saintly, and prayerful life of Jesus Christ, then the sterner world-renouncing features of his life must also find some kind of organized and institutional representation. The Tractarians were disturbed to observe that the Anglican Church of their own day had apparently no saints, and that Anglicanism seemed to water down Christianity to something that seemed more practicable for the average Christian than Christ's own genuine and integral teaching.

Newman went some way to meet this need by his "monastery" at Littlemore, but it remained for Pusey to launch the first monastic Anglican community of women since the Reformation. He looked at it perhaps as a centre of activity rather than as a house of prayer; but it was a courageous venture, and forms a landmark in the history of the Catholic Revival.

In the last hundred years, however, there has been a wonderful revival of monastic life and of religious communities in the Church of England,[10]—surely one of the happiest results of the Oxford Movement. This silent and indomitable rebellion is, without question, one of the most remarkable episodes in the Anglican history of the nineteenth century. Gradually and without any central direction or organization, the ideal of the religious life re-established itself almost spontaneously.

The early communities, though for the most part established in dioceses where the bishop was sympathetic, had no official and recognized place in the life of the Church of England; they had to face much suspicion and, at times, active hostility. But, since 1861 when the movement was first discussed in the Convocation of Canterbury, their contribution to the life of the Church has been increasingly understood, and, as the years passed, relations between the bishops and the growing communities, both of men and women, have gradually improved, and their status has come to receive wider recognition by the Church as a whole. Nowadays the communities receive formal recognition from the authorities of the Church and live with them in a relationship of mutual trust.

The number of women under religious vows and of their communities has always exceeded that of men; at present, there are about two thousand Sisters in the Church of England, and about four hundred men religious, clerics and lay brothers. These numbers are not perhaps very large, but the communities have exercised an influence out of all proportion to their size. They have been centres of prayer and recollection, where Christian people could renew their vision of the reality of God, and they have provided, and still provide, models and patterns of what the liturgical life of the Church might be. The communities of men have played a large part in the recovery of the practice of retreats and in encouraging the movement for parochial missions, while Kelham and Mirfield both direct important colleges for the training of men for the ministry.

In the present century one of the most striking and unexpected developments in the Church of England has been the growth of contemplative communities of women, especially of Benedictine nuns. In an age so activist as our own, which places so much value on external activities and outward possessions, there is a particular need for the witness of those whose activity and treasure are wholly in the inner life.

Another development which began about ten years ago, has been—and is—the flowering of ecumenical activities in the Anglican communities of men and women. Everywhere they have established contact with the monks and nuns of the Roman Catholic and Eastern Orthodox Churches and have found a deep unity with them in their common devotion to God.

IV. ACCEPTANCE OF BIBLICAL CRITICISM AND
OF MODERN SCIENTIFIC KNOWLEDGE

The leaders of the Oxford Movement in its first period, especially Dr Pusey, were conservative in their biblical outlook; they proclaimed the infallibility, the inerrancy, and the verbal inspiration of the whole Bible which, in every part, chapter and verse, was "the Word of God". Their successors in the Catholic Movement, from the 1880s onwards, have been conspicuously ready to accept all the sound and permanent results of contemporary biblical criticism. The first leader of these Liberal Catholics was Charles Gore, bishop first of Birmingham and later, of Oxford.

The great landmark in their courageous change of theological orientation is assuredly the publication in 1889 of *Lux Mundi,* edited by Gore, who was at that time principal of Pusey House; this was also one of the principal crises in the Catholic Revival. It was a crisis in the sense that, whereas this volume was expressly designed "to succour a faith distressed, by endeavouring to bring the Christian Creed into its right relation to the modern growth of knowledge", it produced division within the ranks of the Catholic Movement. Considered as a whole, these essays are a fine exposition of Catholic doctrine on the incarnation, the holy Trinity, the atonement, and the sacraments; all this, of course, was most welcome to the Catholic mind. But one particular essay on the Holy Spirit and Inspiration, by Gore himself, disturbed and divided the supporters of the Catholic Movement. In it Gore accepted in principle the critical theory of inspiration, the modern views of Old Testament criticism, the theory of *kenosis,* namely that of the self-imposed limitations of the knowledge of the Son of God within the human sphere; by so doing he definitely broke with the conservative position of Pusey and the other Tractarians. For this reason *Lux Mundi,* a book of historic importance, caused great distress to many older members of the High Church school.

It is obvious that the position proclaimed by *Lux Mundi* necessarily involved the acceptance of the methods of biblical criticism and of its assured results, in so far as these were really based upon a scientific study of the facts, and not dictated by antimiraculous or anticredal presuppositions. The relief thus bestowed upon the overburdened faith of the educated Christian was immediate and enormous, especially in regard to the Old Testament which had been one of the chief battle-grounds between Christian religion and modern science.

With the admission that the early chapters of Genesis were folklore and poetry, not strictly history, the conflict between the Bible and geology disappeared. The way was thrown open for a possible reconciliation between the scientific hypothesis of Evolution and the traditional Christian doctrine of the Fall. With the abandonment of the idea of verbal inspiration, Balaam's ass and "the sun and moon standing still in the midst of heaven" (Josh. 10. 13), ceased to be stumbling-blocks. The Book of Jonah assumed a new and beautiful character as an allegorical plea for religious universalism when once the status formerly claimed for it, as the literal record of a grotesque wonder, had frankly been surrendered.

But the principle of "proving all things" and accepting modern knowledge in so far as it was knowledge, could not be confined to the domain of the Old Testament. Gore's essay in *Lux Mundi* was, for instance, dealing with the profound, delicate, and embarrassing problem of the nature of the consciousness of Jesus Christ as man, and with the possibility of a kenotic Christology which would safeguard the Catholic doctrine of the incarnation, whilst conceding the possibility of human limitations in the incarnate's knowledge.

Another subsequent work dealt also with the main themes of the Christian and Catholic faith, but gave special attention to the issues raised by recent biblical studies, modern science, and modern philosophy. It was the collective volume, *Essays Catholic and Critical*, edited by Dr E. G. Selwyn, dean of Winchester, and published in 1926. The contributors maintained that the terms "catholic" and "critical" are not antithetical, but stand for two movements which, in union, lead to a deeper understanding of historic Christianity.

In these notable volumes and in other theological, philosophical, and historical works by many eminent Catholic writers, Catholic theology as we understand it is combined with biblical criticism and modern science; it is shown that the two are not irreconcilable. This is a very remarkable change for the better. The Liberal Catholics, as also the Liberal Evangelicals since 1923, were prepared to accept from the biblical scholars of the critical school and to incorporate in their general theological outlook, that which may be called "the assured results of biblical criticism and of modern science". Besides, they were, and are today, also ready to adopt a critical spirit, a free and open attitude towards the world, in every circumstance of their lives and of their intellectual inquiries. This readiness among educated men and women to entertain the critical spirit is one of the most congenial features of the Catholic Revival in the Church of England during this century. Happily this critical approach is not a monopoly of the English Modernists.

V. THE MODERN LITURGICAL REVIVAL

In the second half of the nineteenth century, many men who had been influenced by the Catholic revival, began to take an increasing interest in the forms of worship and in decorous ceremonial to accompany the celebration of the Eucharist. The bishops, the authorities within the Church who might have accepted and guided the Catholic Movement in this country, met this impulse with the same unintelligent denunciation and legalist oppression as their predecessors had shown to the Methodist Movement a century earlier, and tried to suppress it by proceedings in the secular courts and in the Judicial Committee of the Privy Council. Inevitably this episcopal hostility gave rise to a spirit of equally unreasonable defiance among many of the oppressed. But no persecution could break the spirit of such devoted and indomitable London missionary priests as Mackonochie, Lowder, Dolling, Stanton, and others, and the Movement (to which its opponents gave the odious nickname of "Ritualism") continued to survive all the attempts of the Crown, Parliament, and the judiciary to crush it. It succeeded in consolidating its position, conducting its worship with accompaniments of outward beauty, and preaching a clear-cut doctrine suitable for the understanding of those poverty-stricken and common people of the slums among whom most of the "Ritualists" worked.

Between 1846 (the Gorham case) and 1890 (the Lincoln Judgement) a series of cases were brought before the Judicial Committee of the Privy Council dealing with matters of doctrine and ritual, and especially with questions of liturgical vestments; the whole story is too dismal and too long to be recalled here in detail. It is enough to say that, in spite of the frequent judicial decisions against "ritualism", of the personal interventions of Queen Victoria and of Archbishop Tait, and even of Acts of Parliament such as the Public Worship Regulation Act of 1874, the Anglo-Catholics at last won toleration for eucharistic vestments, and for such other Catholic customs as the eastward position, altar lights, the mixed chalice, unleavened bread, and incense.

The spiritual gains of the liturgical Anglo-Catholic recovery were great indeed. The leaders of the Catholic Revival brought back some of the beautiful services of the ancient and medieval Western Church, especially the Holy Week services (Palm Sunday, Maundy Thursday, Good Friday, Easter Vigil). This recovery is nowadays valuable both pastorally and liturgically, since these services in their present form, particularly the Easter Vigil, being biblical and based on primitive practices, do not go outside the basic principles of Anglicanism, to which the restorers remain completely loyal.

Today, three centuries after its publication, all its users (some Conservative Evangelicals excepted) recognize that the 1662 English Book of Common Prayer is out of date, archaic, largely unintelligible in its Tudor vocabulary and phraseology, partly irrelevant for the educated men and women of the twentieth century, and quite unsatisfactory, especially in the matter of its eucharistic theology. Most of the other

Churches and provinces of the Anglican Communion have already revised their Prayer Books; but officially the Church of England still lags far behind the others in this respect. Happily, however, the 1662 Prayer Book is doomed; I suppose that only a few will continue to use it strictly in its present form, especially for the celebration of the Holy Communion.

It was mainly under the pressure of the Catholic Revival in the Church of England, and of the Liturgical Movement in the Roman Catholic Church that at long last after the shock caused by the double rejection in 1927 and 1928 of the revised Prayer Book by the House of Commons, the Church of England decided to entrust to her Liturgical Commission (established in 1954), the preparation of a new Book of Common Prayer. This will not be a mere revision of the obsolete Book of 1662, but a *new* book more understandable by the ordinary people, more relevant to their actual needs, and more in agreement with the assured results of liturgiology.

In December 1965, the Church of England Liturgical Commission published the Alternative Services: Second Series, containing new texts (especially Mattins, Evensong, Burial of the Dead, and Holy Communion) to be introduced to the Convocations and to the House of Laity[11]. A new draft Order of the Holy Communion (the second one) was produced in April 1966 by the same Commission.[12]

Under the pressure of Conservative Evangelicals in the House of Laity, this second draft for the Eucharist was unhappily altered in two important passages: about the prayer for the dead, and the offering of the Bread and Cup. This new rite, the third draft, for the Eucharist was formerly authorized for experimental use in the Church of England for a period not exceeding four years from 7 July 1967.[13]

It is to be hoped that, after a convenient time for experimental use in many churches, the Liturgical Commission will reconsider its findings as to the language and the style—that of the sixteenth and seventeenth centuries—which they have maintained in the new Second Series services. There are still words, expressions, and sentences which are clearly archaic, obsolete, obscure, or of dubious meaning which belong to the English language of four centuries ago.

In particular, the ideal aim of the present revision of the 1662 Book in linguistic matters should be to provide the Church of England with a new wording of her liturgy and mainly of the Eucharist, in a language and phraseology at once noble, hieratical, and liturgical and yet comprehensible, such as can now be found in the new French translation of the Roman Catholic Mass, including the three new eucharistic prayers.

3

The Present Spectrum of the Church

Four main traditions of theology and thought may be found in the Church of England at the present time: the Catholic (formerly the Anglo-Catholic), the Evangelical, the Central, and the Modernist. This classification of the main traditions and schools of thought has become more and more arbitrary, but it is still a useful method of describing the position clearly.

At the present time, however, when so much is in a state of flux, the divisions and cleavages are also changing. New problems arise: some divide churchmen along the old party lines, while others give rise to different alignments and new groupings, in particular the cleavage between Conservatives and Radicals. This can be seen again and again in the proceedings of the Convocations and of the Church Assembly. When, for instance, proposals were made for an organic union between the Church of England and the Methodist Church, it was noticeable that, on the side of the Church of England, the opposition came mainly from the extreme right of the "Catholic tradition" and from the extreme left of the "Evangelical tradition". Another instance is the Parish and People Movement, which gained so much strength that it almost became a tradition of its own. Its roots were in the Catholic Revival, but it gained the support of all those who would like to see the eucharistic liturgy as the central and main service of the Lord's day in every parish.

It would be quite erroneous to put too much emphasis on the idea that these four traditions are complete in themselves and mutually exclusive. Nowadays the same theologian can be at once and with complete honesty—and surely this is the ideal position—Catholic *and* Protestant, Catholic *and* Evangelical, an Evangelical Catholic who is filled with a genuine sympathy for most (not all) of those views which characterize the Modern (or Modernist) Churchmen. As far as I am concerned, I hope to be, and to be called, an Evangelical Catholic.

Therefore it is, from now on, not quite accurate to state categorically and exclusively that the Evangelical party stands for individual conversion and personal piety; that the Modernist party stands for intellectual alertness and the right of free criticism in the light of growing knowledge; that the Central party stands for the *via media*, tolerance, and charity; and that the Catholic party stands for the maintenance of traditional beliefs and values and for the dignity of public worship. These tidy divisions no longer apply to the Anglican scene, at least in England. There is an increasing complexity of Anglican life and thought. The closer mutual contacts and friendly interrelations which exist today are among the happy characteristics of the actual theological situation in the English Church at this present time.

1. CATHOLICS AND EVANGELICALS
TWO GREAT MOVEMENTS

Since the Reformation, there have been in fact two great movements of revival in the Church of England, the Evangelical Revival of the eighteenth century, and the Oxford Movement of the nineteenth. They gave their respective shape to the two principal traditions, the Evangelical and the Catholic, which exist to this day side by side and with great vigour in our Church. Yet both traditions are older than these revivals. Their continuity and homogeneous development can be traced from Reformation times: through Nicholas Ridley, bishop of London, to Charles Simeon (1759-1836); through Lancelot Andrewes, bishop of Winchester, to Bishop Charles Gore (1853-1932); through Nicholas Ferrar of Little Gidding to Richard Meux Benson, the founder of the Society of St John the Evangelist at Cowley (1824-1915). At all periods throughout these centuries, we observe men of great piety and devotion within both traditions: Henry Martyn, the Evangelical missionary (1781-1812) and John Keble, one of the fathers of the Oxford Movement (1792-1866); Charles Simeon, one of the main leaders of the Evangelical Revival and Edward Bouverie Pusey, the outstanding Tractarian leader (1800-82); James Hannington, the Evangelical bishop of East Equatorial Africa (1847-85) and Frank Weston, the Anglo-Catholic bishop of Zanzibar (1871-1924). Yet the differences between each pair of men seem to disappear, when contrasted with the Christ-centred devotion which enlivened them all.

Other Churches also can show equally striking contrasts in holiness, but it is difficult to imagine so great a diversity of types of devotion attaining such fullness of spiritual stature, except within the Church of England, or within the Roman Catholic Church of the post-Tridentine period, when the various "schools of spirituality" had differing characteristics, yet were not mutually exclusive. The remarkable feature of the different types of devotion, shown by various saintly men of the Church of England, is not the tenacity with which each holds to his particular tradition, but their common devotion to Christ. This devotion has always grown, and still grows, out of the love and study of the Scriptures, and out of an affectionate adherence to the piety of the Book of Common Prayer. Neither the Catholic nor the Evangelical type of Anglican holiness can be explained in terms of a practical *via media,* or of a Church which is committed to some form of Anglo-Saxon compromise.

It is not easy to describe the two greater Anglican traditions, the Catholic or the Evangelical, any more than the two lesser, the Central and the Modernist. There are happily no formal definitions; changes of nomenclature and of emphasis constantly occur, and all the traditions in our Church are living and growing; they are not static or embalmed.

2. NEW FACTORS AND NEW GROUPINGS
CONSERVATIVES AND RADICALS

Nowadays the four traditional schools are increasingly living in a state of co-existence, at peace with each other, and friendly towards each other. The dividing walls between them are happily everywhere crumbling; partisanship is everywhere decreasing. The bitterness and animosity which marked the theological disputes of the nineteenth century, have become a matter for quiet historical study and, among all responsible theologians, an occasion for shame and regret. The essentials of the common faith are coming to be recognized in their right perspective. Of course, disputes on theological matters go on, but with less violence and rancour than in the past, and with a greater reverence for the susceptibilities of men of other persuasions.

Another important matter to which I have already referred is the way in which the traditional pattern of Anglicanism is being subjected to deep and thoroughgoing alteration. New factors and new groupings have emerged in recent years, over the whole field of the activities of the comprehensive Church of England. Especially, since the publication of such books as *Soundings* (1962), edited by Dr Alec Vidler,[1] and *Honest to God* (1963) by Dr John Robinson, then bishop of Woolwich[2], it is manifest that the growing and main cleavage within the Church of England is no longer between Catholics and Evangelicals but between Conservative and Radical Christians. This new rift cuts right across all the former parties and theological tendencies.

Both sides, the Conservative and the Radical, will have to learn the difficult art of living together in peace and charity, and of learning from each other. The new lines of demarcation are now taking shape— not only in England—on a new pattern, different from those which once divided the Catholic party from the Evangelical. Many members of the former Catholic and Evangelical parties are nowadays united in commending and praising a movement symbolized by the former Bishop of Woolwich's recent Book, *The New Reformation?*,[3] a movement which seems to them to be the coming of a new and radical reformation of the Church, while members of the same two parties, people of traditional views, are found united to oppose it. Now and in the near future, there will be an intense, and at times passionate, conflict between the Traditionalists or Conservatives and the Innovators or Radicals. Within the next ten or twenty years, the theologians of the Church of England will have to work out some method by which these two new and powerful tendencies—this new "left" and "right"— within her can hold together in peace, mutual tolerance, and loving fellowship. The same is true of all the other great Christian Churches, and not least of the Roman Catholic Church, since the Second Vatican Council.

3. THE CATHOLIC TRADITION AND IDEAL

The loyal Catholics of the Church of England regard their Church not only as a continuance of the medieval ecclesiastical tradition in this country, but as a truly Catholic and comprehensive Church, and a living part of the holy, catholic, and apostolic Church. Their Church, which is the legitimate Catholic Church in England, provides them with the Christian faith and life in all its fullness, a fullness combining things new and old, and leaving ample room for further progress under the guidance of the Spirit of truth.

For them, Catholicism is not just one of the elements in Christianity; rather, it is Christianity at its richest and fullest. At its best it attaches a fundamental importance to the institutional and social elements in Christianity, as well as to the intellectual, personal, and mystical. There is no element of positive value in any truly Christian school of thought which is alien to genuine Catholicism, and cannot find a place in Catholic thought and life. One cannot repeat too often that every true Catholic is bound to be also a true Evangelical. There cannot be any truly Christian life, except on the basis of personal conversion and discipleship, of repentance towards God, and faith in our Lord Jesus Christ. Catholicism, at its best, includes all the positive values on which Evangelicals rightly lay stress, but it sets them in a fuller perspective and in a more social institutional context, and so preserves them in a more just proportion.

The same applies with regard to the claims of the intellect. In so far as the Modernist school of thought has championed these claims, it has done useful work and borne faithful witness to the truth. In so far as the radical movement (of which *Honest to God* is the manifesto) is now presenting the case for the acceptance of extensive changes in theological statements and in ecclesiastical organization, it may be compatible with Catholic orthodoxy. In so far as this radical movement tries to satisfy the intellectual needs and aspirations of secularized man (granted that it is always keeping within the limits of Catholic orthodoxy), it is also doing good service. To this extent, even *Honest to God* bears witness to the abundant richness and the many facets of the Christian and Catholic truth.

It is a matter for deep regret that in past years—and not only in the Church of England, but more markedly in the Roman Catholic Church —Catholic orthodoxy appeared to be rigid, timidly traditional, and afraid to face new knowledge whether in the sphere of natural science or of biblical and historical scholarship. Wherever this has been the case it was not because orthodoxy was Catholic, but because it was not sufficiently Catholic. I have already observed that, if the first leaders of the Oxford Movement regarded "liberalism" as the main enemy, their successors as the Catholic Movement developed, were marked by a truly liberal outlook as their influence expanded and succeeded. The greatest landmark in the work of reconciliation between the claims of the new modern critical science and those of the traditional Catholic faith, was in England the publication of *Lux Mundi* by Gore and the other successors of the Tractarians, rather than *Essays and Reviews*, which was published in 1860 by a number of Broad Churchmen or mild rationalists of that day.

Anyone who wishes to understand quickly how Catholic thought in the Church of England has moved should study two books: *Essays Catholic and Critical* (1926)[4] and a much smaller work *Catholicity* (1947)[5] prepared at the request of the then archbishop of Canterbury, Lord Fisher. He will see that, at the time of the publication of *Lux Mundi* (1889), the acceptance of the findings of modern critical scholarship appeared to be a rash innovation, but it was taken for granted by all the thinkers who contributed to the two later books. Their aim was not so much the defence of one particular point of view as the search for true Catholicity, of *wholeness* or fullness of Christian faith and life.

It is true that the Catholic Movement in England has suffered from being judged by isolated by-products. Many sincere Christians, even some members of the Church of England, continue to see in it nothing more than a reactionary traditionalism or to regard it as exclusively concerned with liturgical forms and ceremonies.

There are still some traditionalist Anglo-Catholic priests of the old school whose conservative views are shown in many ways, but especially in liturgical and "ritualistic" matters. Even today, they seem to attach great importance to the wearing of ugly vestments of the so-called "Roman" shape, even when they might replace them with others of more beautiful form. They seem very happy to retain just those vestments and ceremonial practices which are being suppressed or discouraged, wholly or in part, by the present Liturgical Movement in the Roman Catholic Church, especially since the Second Vatican Council. In particular, they are very anxious to maintain in their churches the extra-liturgical devotions in honour of the Blessed Sacrament. These nostalgic Anglo-Catholic priests do not desire to see any *radical* departure from "our own incomparable liturgy" of the 1662 Book of Common Prayer. They are sufficiently satisfied with the insertion of some "Catholic" rites and prayers as "propers".

On the other hand, there are many young Anglican Catholics or Catholic Anglicans, priests and laymen, who nowadays proudly call themselves Catholics, but who are not fully at ease with their liberal Catholic brethren and are becoming more radical than they. These intellectuals plead—and at times clamour—for the general acceptance of big changes in theological statements, in ecclesiastical structures, machinery, and organization. These radical Catholic Anglicans of today are not by any means all angry young men. Their ideas seem now to be spreading among the whole Catholic Movement and exercise a powerful influence. Provided that they remain faithful to the genuine reality of the Catholic faith, and provided that they combine their radical views and aspirations with a wide outlook and a supra-national concern for ecumenical problems and activities, they will contribute no doubt to the widening of the Catholic vision. Their mentality is neither insular nor imbued with self-complacency.[6]

4. THE EVANGELICAL TRADITION AND IDEAL

In the Church of England, the term "Evangelical" is currently applied to the school of thought or theological tradition which lays special stress on personal conversion and personal salvation by a faith focusing on the atoning death of our Saviour Jesus Christ. This is not the place to recall the history of Anglican Evangelicalism. Some names and dates will suffice.

The group, which was the successor and heir of the Puritans of the sixteenth and seventeenth centuries, originated in the eighteenth century to bring reality into religion when Christian life in England was at its lowest ebb, and when the clergymen were too often negligent and worldly. The Evangelical group had several points of close contact with the Methodist Movement, especially in the more Calvinistic form of George Whitefield; but it sought to work on the basis of the Anglican parochial system and never contemplated separation from the Church of England. Among its leaders in the eighteenth century were John Fletcher, Henry Venn, William Romaine, and John Newton. To a rather later date belonged Charles Simeon (1759-1836), who established the Evangelical tradition at Cambridge, and the influential laymen of the so-called Clapham Sect, of whom William Wilberforce was the most famous. Dislike of their religious earnestness led to much opposition from diverse quarters. But their piety, zeal, and humanity gradually won them a large following. In the nineteenth century they took a leading part in missionary work and social reform, such as the abolition of slavery and the introduction of the Factory Acts.

Theologically, the Evangelicals of the eighteenth and nineteenth centuries, and the Conservative Evangelicals of this century, have generally upheld the verbal inspiration, inerrancy, and sole authority of Scripture (*Sola Scriptura*), denying that the Church—even the universal Church—has power to impose her interpretation upon the judgement of the individual believer. They stressed, and still stress, the supreme importance of preaching with, as a correlative, a low view of liturgical worship and of the theology of the sacraments. They maintained, and maintain to this day, a deeply rooted suspicion of the Roman Catholic Church, and a marked hostility to characteristic Tractarian and so-called High Church doctrines and practices. On the other hand, they were, and are, profoundly convinced of the sinfulness of man, of his inability to save himself, and of his need for a personal Saviour. For them God is not an abstract Idea, but the God who cares, the God who has acted in history, the God who, in Jesus Christ, has met, and still meets, man with provision for his every need. Man's response must be through obedience and holiness.

In the first years of this century differences arose amongst the Evangelicals, between their more conservative and their more liberal members; these divisions came to a head when, in 1922, some of the strict Conservatives discontinued their support of the Church Missionary Society and formed the Bible Churchmen's Missionary Society. The split struck the Evangelical cause at its most sensitive point, but probably the rift was bound to appear. By now there are two groups within the Evangelical tradition: the Conservative Evangelicals and the Liberal Evangelicals.

5. THE CONSERVATIVE EVANGELICALS

Like their predecessors of past centuries, the Conservative Evangelicals of today continue to emphasize the sole authority of the Bible (*Sola Scriptura*) in contrast to the emphasis placed by the Catholics upon the Church and her dogmatic Tradition as well as the Bible. So most of them, with their representative theologians, continue to assert that they cannot do justice to this view without believing in the verbal inspiration, the literal inerrancy, and the infallibility of the Scriptures. They proclaim that, according to the New Testament, not only the biblical writers, but also all their books and all their words were inspired; that there are no degrees of inspiration, because all the Bible is, alike and in all its parts, the Word of God; and that all the biblical books, even the so-called historical ones, are equally inspired, infallible, and authoritative.[7]

The Conservative Evangelical uses biblical terms and phraseology to express his faith and his peculiar theology, which is predominantly Calvinistic. He accepts the dogmatic Tradition of the Church, in so far as he is satisfied that the traditional creeds and the other pronouncements of the Councils "may be proved by most certain warrants of Holy Scripture" (Article 8). But he distrusts all ecclesiastical, liturgical, and canonical customs and traditions which cannot be so proved or tested by most certain warrants of Holy Scripture. Of course, he has a very high regard for the Thirty-nine Articles as finally promulgated in 1571. These seem to him to be the immutable doctrinal standard of the Church of England, and he interprets them in accordance with a genuine and strong Reformed theology, for they are for him the "domestic Creed" for the English Church. He is convinced not only that they are agreeable to the Word of God, but also that every clergyman of the Church of England can, and should, assent to them with a good conscience.[8]

Like their predecessors, Conservative Evangelicals are profoundly convinced of the sinfulness and total depravity of man, of his inability to redeem himself before God, and of his urgent need for a personal Saviour who is Jesus Christ himself. They think that all Anglican clergy, whatever their views on other matters, should unite in teaching not only an Augustinian and Calvinistic doctrine of sin, but also a Reformed doctrine of justification by faith alone and of divine grace; in other words, the interpretation of the New Testament adopted by the Reformers of the sixteenth century. Their stress on the doctrine of justification by faith alone is very strong indeed.[9] Both the Conservative and the Liberal Evangelicals insist that our acceptance by God depends solely on faith and a complete reliance on his promise of complete salvation. To believe means to commit our needs and our sins wholly to our Advocate Jesus Christ who is the propitiation for our sins. The natural corollary to the doctrine of justification by faith is that of the assurance of salvation. The Christian who relies on Jesus Christ for salvation is undoubtedly saved. But the evidence of his faith, which brings assurance, depends on a life of communion with God.

Like the Catholic, the Conservative Evangelical exalts the cross and Christ's death upon it as the sole means of man's salvation, but he likes to argue that Christ died in man's place to satisfy God's justice, giving thus to his Father a sufficient vicarious satisfaction for the sins of the whole world. But this particular theory of personal substitution is not an exclusive view; it is rather a strong emphasis thrown on a theological doctrine.

The Conservative Evangelical also emphasizes the work of the Holy Spirit to bring about a new birth of the sinner who, by grace, is a believer, and he applies the same emphasis equally to the work of the Spirit in the growth of the individual as to the spiritual rebirth or personal conversion, another essential theme.

Like the Free Churches in England and the Protestant Churches overseas, Conservative Evangelicals stress the ministry of preaching and the universal priesthood of all believers, putting the preaching and the hearing of the Word of God before the sacramental faith and practice. Though they reject asceticism, they maintain for the individual a high, and at times austere, standard of personal morality and holiness. They reject the doctrines of baptismal regeneration and of the eucharistic sacrifice, as they are taught and accepted in the Orthodox and the Roman Catholic Churches.

It is regrettable that many Conservative Evangelicals still persist in their mistrust of the Roman Catholic Church. Some of them are not yet prepared to recognize the enormous change of atmosphere within that Church today, or the positive values of the agonizing reappraisal which she is now undertaking as a consequence of the Second Vatican Council. Some of them seem also to take the same negative view of the present Ecumenical Movement.

It was, however, immensely heartening to see that, on these two subjects, namely the Roman Catholic Church and the World Council of Churches, as well as on many other important subjects, the National Evangelical Congress, held at Keele University in April 1967, took a more open, sympathetic, and friendly attitude.

Nowadays the English Conservative Evangelicals appear to be more ready to listen to others and to enter with them in a fruitful dialogue, especially with the other Anglicans. Indeed among the major emphases at Keele, was a stress on an orthodox and living theology, and on the desire to take a responsible part in the corporate life of the Church of England. Also the members of the Congress recognized that all the Christians, including Evangelicals, must show the implications of the gospel for the social, moral, and international problems of our time.[10]

6. THE LIBERAL EVANGELICALS

More liberal ideas appeared within the Evangelical group at the beginning of this century, splitting it and giving birth to a new body of broad-minded Evangelicals ready to be more sacramental, more scholarly, and more eirenic in outlook. The clergy and laymen who share these views still maintain their spiritual descent from the Evangelical Revival, but they are concerned to restate old truths, especially about the authority of the Bible, the atonement, and the Church, in terms which they think more consonant with modern science and its stress on the historical method, and with the philosophy of personality.

In 1906 a private body, with the title of "Group Brotherhood", arose from the desire of the younger Evangelicals to free Evangelicalism from what they regarded as an unduly conservative interpretation of Christianity and in particular of the Bible. They welcomed the help of science and criticism in the search for truth, and wished to infuse more dignity and beauty into worship. In 1923 this group adopted the title of "The Anglican Evangelical Group Movement" and, under the leadership of V. F. Storr, canon of Westminster, became a powerful association of Anglican clergy and laity, holding Liberal Evangelical views, and pledged to study the social and economic implications of the gospel and to work for effective unity among all Christian people. It ceased to exist as a distinct entity in 1967.

This new type of Evangelicalism was neither liberal nor conservative in the earlier sense of these terms. It was entirely open to the ideas and methods of modern scholarship; it was not greatly interested in the old controversies about ritual and ceremonial. It continued to stand firm in the biblical tradition of the English Reformers and the

Evangelical divines, with their emphasis on justification by faith alone, on the obligation to lead a holy life, and on the Christian assurance through the work of the Holy Spirit. In 1950 seventeen representatives of this school of thought published a small book entitled: *The Fulness of Christ: The Church's Growth into Catholicity;*[11] this remarkable statement of the Liberal Evangelical position is parallel to the Anglo-Catholic statement, *Catholicity,* of 1947.

In general, Liberal Evangelicals were and are anxious to restate biblical doctrines in modern terms, provided that this can be done without affecting the integrity of Christian orthodoxy (as interpreted in the Evangelical manner), and with the customary Evangelical emphases. As far as the Bible is concerned, they resemble the Liberal Catholics and are unable to accept the verbal inspiration, the literal inerrancy, and the infallibility of the Scriptures. They know that the Bible is a collection, not of oracles, but of ancient documents of different dates, in which it is easy to discover many historical inaccuracies. But they know also that the quality which gives to this collection its religious grandeur, its perennial attraction, and its legitimate claim on our attention, is that the Bible's subject is the activity of God in the redemption of mankind, his activity towards man, and his progressive disclosure of himself to man. For the Liberal Evangelical theologian (as for every reasonable and sober Christian theologian) the numerous books of the Bible—in particular those of the New Testament—provide him with the evidence for the acts of God towards mankind, but they are not manuals of ethics or text-books of theology. This book, though not inerrant, impresses powerfully all who study it, and possesses a unique religious meaning.[12]

It goes without saying that the Liberal Evangelicals maintain, like all Anglicans, the authority of the Bible as the normative and decisive record of the historic Christian revelation, and as the standard of the Church's faith.

Further, the Liberal Evangelicals do not accept the Conservative Evangelicals' tenet that the basic principle for the interpretation of Christ's redemptive work, by his sacrifice on the cross, is that of penal substitution. Against this Calvinistic view, they put emphasis upon the cross as the supreme example of God's love, rather than of his justice, which demands the penal substitution of his innocent Son.[13]

7. THE TRADITION OF CENTRAL CHURCHMANSHIP

It is obvious that the present spectrum of the Church of England includes, between the Catholic and the Evangelical traditions, the comparatively modern tradition of Central Churchmanship. By definition this tradition is neither Catholic nor Evangelical, but offers a kind of practical *via media* or moderate type of Churchmanship. In fact, a Central Churchman has a bias, often unconscious, towards one or other tradition; many of them are rather Evangelical and others rather Catholic. Some are more Evangelical than the Catholics, but not so Evangelical as the Evangelicals; others are more Catholic than the Evangelicals, but not so Catholic as the Catholics. It is manifest that the Central Churchmen cannot achieve the impossible feat of being exactly central and of preserving a perfect balance.

I am convinced that, in spite of their present numerical importance and their common-sense "moderation", those who hold to the Central tradition will not play any decisive part in the future growth of Anglicanism, or in the vital development of the Church of England in the remaining decades of this century.

Indeed, in spite of appearances, Central Churchmen have never set before them as their goal the maintenance of a precise theological position in the Anglican spectrum, half-way between the Catholics and the Evangelicals. Rather their first objective has always been to avoid the acerbity and bitterness of the theological controversies of their times. As men of common sense, "moderate" and tolerant, they made, and still make, their protest against the failures and partisanship of the other two traditions.

In the Victorian era the churchmen involved in destructive controversies were not always the only people responsible for such harshness and lack of charity. These furious and fruitless disputes often arose from the Erastian principles and jurisprudence of the English law of that time and from the official maxims and practices of the national Church. It is true also that, once a controversial issue has been raised, churchmen of all traditions, as well as people outside the Church, have always been ready to throw fuel on the fire. Thus there have been times, even in this century (as witness the Prayer Book controversy) when men of good will could reasonably regard both Catholics and Evangelicals as dangerous extremists, only fiercely competing with each other for control of the Anglican Church. Both parties are largely responsible for their respective public images as fanatics and extremists, because of their ineptness, lack of mutual charity, and failure to try to understand each other.

In avoiding what they deemed to be extremist positions and un-English fanaticism, Central Churchmen have been faced with the subtle temptation of thinking themselves to be the only true Anglicans.

Further, they have been tempted to adopt a kind of compromise approach in matters of theology, so as to avoid what they thought to be the Catholic and Evangelical "extremes". Their unconscious reaction, of which they have not always been aware, has been to support the tradition which seemed at the time to be losing ground, and so to re-establish the balance between the contending "parties".

The situation and prospects of the Central Churchmen today have changed. Neither the Catholic nor the Evangelical tradition did much to check the growing forces of secularism and materialism or to guide the development of the Welfare State into the Affluent Society. Lacking one or the other of their strong and accustomed influences for action or reaction, the Central Churchmen had little to offer, and what they had was not sufficiently positive to provide any effective protest. Therefore outsiders (especially young people) began to look on the Church of England as a pleasant anachronism and an honourable irrelevancy, worthy of preservation not because of her message of salvation or of her redeeming truth, but because of her historical and sentimental links with the glorious national past which was rapidly receding.

In these conditions, I doubt whether the Central tradition of churchmanship can survive much longer in its present form. The doctrines which are common to it and the other traditions, are challenged and rejected by the materialist and secularized society of today. The radicals and the humanists look for authoritative and unequivocal answers to their blunt questions; these answers must contain clear statements, especially as to the nature of the authority which is claimed by the universal or the national Church. In so far as the Central Churchman holds the rather negative position of protest against either the Catholic or the Evangelical, he is unable to give any clear answer, for he is undecided in his definitions of the nature and the seat of authority in either the universal or his national Church.[14]

May I end this section on a more personal note? Whether he knows it or not, the Central churchman in the Church of England is an Anglo-Saxon who inclines towards compromise in all matters of theology, worship, and action. The man who seeks such a compromise between what he thinks to be the two extremes, namely the poles of Catholicism and Evangelicalism, not only has to steer a difficult course between their supposed errors and excesses; he will also miss or ignore the great spiritual values of the two spiritual poles. Any compromise in religious matters has characteristic defects and corruptions of its own. The real trouble about this practical *via media* is its chronic tendency towards complacency and mediocrity. The moderate man, trying pragmatically to steer this middle course, may end up in an unlovely mood of self-conceit which is in no way justified by his middle position. In so far as Central churchmen occupy this "moderate" position of compromise in matters of religion, they cannot show either the breadth or the depth of the Anglican synthesis, of its meeting and merging of all the living values of Catholicism and Evangelicalism. In fact, the Anglican who prefers this pragmatic "middle" is farther from the Anglican vision than either the uncompromising Catholic or the uncompromising Evangelical. The "no-party party" is the worst of all "parties", theological and ecclesiastical, and in all other matters.

One of the main theses of this book is to emphasize that the ideal and the mission, in God's providence, of the Anglican Communion lies in the close union and the hopeful collaboration for the future of the out-and-out Evangelicals, and of the out-and-out Catholics, and not in an eventual triumph of Central churchmanship.

8. THE MODERNISTS

The Modernist Movement in the Church of England expresses its views mainly through the Modern Churchmen's Union, a society founded in 1898 and called (until 1908) the Churchmen's Union, for the advancement of liberal Christian thought, especially within the Church of England. Its main aims are to uphold the wide comprehensiveness of the Church of England, and to maintain therein the legitimacy of the restatement of doctrines, and the need to adjust the forms of public worship in accordance with the requirements of modern science and modern thought.

The aims of the Modernist Movement are officially and authoritatively set out on the cover-page of the recent numbers of the Movement's journal, *The Modern Churchman,* and I quote them *verbatim.*

The objects of the Union are:

To affirm the progressive character of God's self-revelation and the certainty that no truth can lead away from him.

To proclaim Christ and his Gospel in the light of modern knowledge, endeavouring to give a clear meaning of all phrases which are open to ambiguous statement.

To maintain the right and duty of the Church of England to reject what is false, and to restate what is true in her traditional dogmas.

To defend the freedom of responsible students, clerical as well as lay, in their work of criticism and research.

To secure more regard for beauty and truth in church services, and the use of language and customs in harmony with modern thought.

To promote the application of Christian principles in public as well as in private life.

To assert the right and duty of the laity to take a due share in the government and work of the Church.

To maintain the historic comprehensiveness of the Church of England, and to foster the movement towards unity among Christians.

The Modernist Movement has disagreed—and still disagrees—with the Anglo-Catholics on some specific matters, such as the pastoral care of people who have been divorced and seek to be remarried in church, and the priestly ordination of women. Its members are not in principle deeply hostile to the Roman Catholic Church, but they are opposed to the particular type of Roman Catholicism in this country which is expressed in the clerical policy emanating from Westminster; this is a very important qualification. In recent years some leading Modernist theologians have questioned, and even attacked, in *The Modern Churchman,* the "South Bank Religion", of which the former bishop of Woolwich, Dr John Robinson, is one of the main representatives.

Their journal, *The Modern Churchman,* is an influential periodical, which has always shown a high standard of critical scholarship. Its founder (in 1911) and first editor was Dr H. D. A. Major, who was, from 1919 to 1948, principal of Ripon Hall, Oxford. The best account of the theological position of the Movement is still to be found in Dr Major's *English Modernism: Its Origin, Methods, Aims* (1927)[15], from which I quote:

The tendency of English Modernism is scientific and historical. Christianity is for it a growing spiritual experience, deepened, strengthened, purified, by worship and obedience—a religion both of redemption and illumination. The Modernist values the Church, but he does not value it for its authority, as does the Catholic, because the supreme authority for the Modernist is not that of the Church but of the Spirit. He values the Church for its social life, its accumulated and treasured spiritual experience, the inspiration of its historic continuity, and its missionary potentiality. The Church is for him the chief agent for extending the Kingdom of God on earth; the principal *organon* through which the process of the Divine Incarnation operates in human history.

The outlook of the Modern Churchmen's Union during its heyday (1920-30) can be summed up in the words of the "Modernist Creed", drawn up by Dr Major himself, which ran as follows:

We believe that God is Spirit, and they that worship him must worship him in Spirit and in truth.

We believe that God is Light, and that, if we walk in the light, as he is in the light, we have fellowship one with another.

We believe that God is Love, and that everyone that loveth is born of God and knoweth God.

We believe that Jesus is the Son of God, and that God hath given to us eternal life, and that life is in his Son.

We believe that we are children of God, and that he hath given us of his Spirit.

We believe that, if we confess our sins, he is faithful and just to forgive us our sins.

We believe that the world passeth away and the lust thereof, but that he that doeth the will of God abideth for ever.[16]

The reader must have noticed that all controversial issues are omitted from this "Modernist Creed", and that Roman Catholics, Anglicans, Protestants, and even Unitarians and Quakers, could unite in repeating it. Those Christians who are faithfully attached to the so-called Nicene Creed will point out that the Virgin Birth, which the Modernists regard as something unhistorical, and the fact of the physical Resurrection of Jesus, are not even mentioned in this "Creed". The same may be said of the descent into Hades, of the ascension into heaven, and of the session at the right hand of God. Neither is there any reference to the resurrection of the flesh, to the return of Jesus in glory to judge the living and the dead, and to the one, holy, catholic, and apostolic Church.

On the other hand, it does not contain any mention of the so-called Protestant dogmas. For instance, there is no reference to holy Scripture and its infallibility and authority, to the Calvinistic doctrine of pre-destination and election, to the Lutheran interpretation of justification by faith alone, to the number of the sacraments (two and no more), to the right of national Churches to govern themselves without outside interference from the Pope or anyone else.

Dr Major contended that, owing to the wording of his Modernist Creed, the old traditional lines of the Christian position had been shortened and drastically straightened, but the doctrinal position of Christianity was maintained intact in its essentials. Whether this assertion is true is precisely the question.

May I end this section with some personal reflections? It is probable that the Modernist Movement had inevitably to appear in the Church of England and that it has had a beneficial effect. It developed—and is still developing—a deliberate effort to protect and promote the right of free theological inquiry, to use the findings of the modern sciences with sympathy, and to insist that there is a development in the understanding of Christian faith.

But the movement which we call English Modernism and which was so strong in the twenties and thirties, has become of decreasing importance, because its peculiar virtues are obviously not the monopoly of one "party" or one theological school, and they have gradually became diffused, here, there, and almost everywhere, in the English Church, except of course among the Conservative Evangelicals. Happily the pursuit of critical study of the Bible, or of a peaceful confrontation between the Christian faith and the modern sciences, is in no way the monopoly of any school of theology.

In spite of the high level of scholarship to be found in *The Modern Churchman*, and in spite of the theological importance of the stimulating debates at its recent annual conferences, the Modernist Movement is nowadays for many reasons restricted to a few intellectual personalities. One reason is that the moral, spiritual, intellectual, and cultural conditions of today, as well outside the Church of England as within her, call insistently for a restatement and re-interpretation of the Christian faith and life in the context of a strongly developed piety and ecclesiastical discipline.

The Modernist does not lack moral courage or intellectual honesty, but he is a born individualist and has never been a great supporter of traditional spirituality or ecclesiastical discipline; he thus has not got the necessary background, without which such a restatement and re-interpretation cannot be fully coherent and articulated. Another reason is that, under the influence of the more radical forms of theological liberalism (symbolized by the Cambridge "New Theology" and especially by the best-seller, *Honest to God*), there has been a kind of counter-reaction with unexpected consequences. Catholics and Evangelicals—even Conservative Evangelicals—have drawn more closely together within the Church, and are being obliged to rediscover their common ground, especially in matter of the Catholic faith. Many theologians and responsible laymen of a traditional cast of mind suspect, quite wrongly, that the former bishop of Woolwich, Dr Robinson, is a Modernist of a peculiar type. This is, I know, untrue; the Bishop is certainly not a member of the Modern Churchmen's Union, and he has been strongly attacked in *The Modern Churchman*. But many people remain doubtful about the Bishop's position, and Dr Robinson's name is still often associated with the English Modernists. This confusion may, at least for some time, hinder the growth of modernist ideas in the present Church of England.

4

The Spectrum Analysed

The bond which ties together practising Anglicans (whether members of the Church of England or of the other Churches and Provinces of the Anglican Communion), cannot be any common loyalty to the Scriptures, for they are not the exclusive possession of any individual Christian Church; nor is it the legal "Establishment" of the Church of England or the close links which have always existed between that Church, and the history, life, and political constitution of the English people. The proof that such an answer is insufficient lies in the fact that the Anglican Communion is world-wide.[1] Of all the Churches and provinces which make up this Communion, only one Church, that of England with its Provinces of Canterbury and York, is "established by law". In Scotland, where it is known as the Scottish Episcopal Church, the Anglican Church can even be "nonconformist" and yet remain Anglican. In many parts of the world the members of the Anglican Communion are only a minority, and, in some places, only a tiny minority, of Christian believers.

Also the Anglican Communion now includes many Churches whose members who are not, even remotely, of English origin, and whose history and culture are not necessarily connected with the past history of the Church of England. The Anglican Church in Burma grows steadily more Burmese and eastern; that in Nigeria, steadily more African. Wherever the Anglican Communion is planted, the local Church becomes increasingly more of an indigenous Church, and less of a transplant, using a liturgy in some language other than English, in a local setting. Yet all these Churches—African and Australian, Indian, Japanese, Polynesian and so on—[2] remain in formal communion with each other. They cherish their common Anglicanism based on the biblical and Catholic faith; they regard Canterbury as their focal point and its archbishop as their *Primus* and the natural chairman of all pan-Anglican assemblies.

We may well ask by what positive bond are the practising members of the Church of England held together? The answer, it would seem, is that, in her present state of *symbiosis* or peaceful and vital co-existence, the Church of England, as also the Anglican Communion, is linked internally by a unity of spirit or ethos.

Practising Anglicans, both in England and elsewhere, feel that they belong together to a particular Church and thence to a particular world-wide Communion. They feel that this religious fellowship with each other is a precious possession and a gift which they are determined to preserve. Yet this unity is essentially a unity in diversity, overriding many differences, and it would lose all its spiritual value, if, by any remote chance, every difference was to disappear. This is not to say that some differences, for instance in theological and liturgical matters, ought not to disappear; and it would no doubt be better if there was more agreement, more of a common mind, more consciousness of belonging to a more united Church of England, which could act more efficiently in the unifying work of the Ecumenical Movement. But in such a case the Church of England would no longer be what she is, and here we are trying to understand the Church of England as she exists today, as a sociological phenomenon.

This practical unity of spirit or ethos, which should be clearly distinguished from the unity in faith, is illustrated by the fact that within the Anglican Communion, and in particular in the Church of England, the colours of the theological spectrum are not clearly divided, but run in an unbroken series of shaded hues from one extreme to the other. The non-Anglican (especially the Roman Catholic and the Orthodox) may be misled by the mention of "wings", "parties", and "traditions" in the Church of England. In fact the great majority of Anglican priests and laymen, both in England and overseas, do not consider themselves as belonging to any particular party. They cluster in large numbers round a vague, central, and practical position which defies logical definition, but whose particular Anglican flavour is clearly recognizable. Here I am not speaking of the faith of the Church. Their numbers thin out noticeably at the two extreme ends: to the right, where is found the Papalist group, and on the left at the extreme Conservative Evangelical fringe. An ordinary Anglican may move in one direction or othe other during his lifetime and may cross over from one theological position to another; he may even go enthusiastically to one or other extreme. Yet he remains at all times within the Anglican fold.

1. PRACTICAL UNITY BASED ON COMMON WORSHIP

We come to ask the question: What is it that, in practice, all committed members of the Church of England and of the Anglican Communion overseas have in common? The answer probably lies in the field of their public and common worship, rather than of explicit and clearly defined dogma or of a common and accepted theology. The practical tie binding them together is fundamentally the Book of Common Prayer considered as the norm of their worship and as the criterion of their corporate Christian life. In the last resort, a responsible Anglican in England is a man who attends his church and there uses the form of public worship or liturgy provided in the Prayer Book of 1662 or even of 1928, or who now uses the radically revised Alternative Series, Second Series, which were approved in 1967 and 1968 by the supreme legislative authority of the Church. Outside England he is a man who attends his church, and there uses one of the family of liturgies sprung from Cranmer's First (1549) or Second (1552) Prayer Books.

In any case, the priest or officiating minister may modify the official or "legal" Prayer Book of the Church in question, because of the deficiencies, irrelevancies, and shortcomings of the 1662 Book. Though any cleric or layman may differ from other Anglicans as to the right interpretation of certain formulas and rubrics of the Eucharistic rite of 1662; yet if he uses either as celebrant or worshipper the official or the alternative Prayer Book of his own Anglican Church, he is truly an Anglican. Equally, if he refuses to use it, there is no legitimate place for him in the Anglican fellowship. This applies, of course, not only to the Eucharist, but also to the other Prayer Book services.

But we must avoid the error of exaggerating or overstating the continuing value and efficacy of the Book of Common Prayer as a unifying force. Undoubtedly the 1662 Book has played an incomparable part in the fashioning of practical unity in the Church. It has moulded the Anglican religious outlook, ethos, and piety, and has given Anglicans a *lex orandi,* in which their *lex credendi* has been expressed in a liturgical phraseology. Men of all "parties", and of none, have given to it their whole-hearted and devout allegiance, but as recent church history shows, everybody in the Church now freely admits that the 1662 Book has failed to remain the bond of unity that it once was. Faced with the actual situation of the Church in our materialistic, secularized, and "desacralized" society, even the Conservative Evangelicals agree in this. When the Catholic Movement started a century ago, its leaders were content to use the 1662 Book, deeming it capable of a Catholic interpretation. But gradually they sought a richer liturgical and devotional use, and the practice of supplementing the Prayer Book from other sources, mainly from the Roman Missal and even the Roman Breviary, became common.

It cannot be denied that the 1662 Book still contains the theological and devotional tradition which it taught to countless Anglicans, but we cannot today claim with honesty that this book is an effective authority for unity in public worship and official teaching; this is one reason why a radical revision of this antiquated Prayer Book was so urgently needed. But no revised Prayer Book, even the "Alternative Services, Second Series", is likely to command the same binding authority as the former "legal" Book had.

The Prayer Book Ordinal of 1662 has been used—as it still is in many places—in its original text or with only slight variations in the Church of England and in the other Churches and provinces of the Anglican Communion. This common use proclaims the continued Catholicity of the Anglican Communion. The threefold ministry of bishops, priests, and deacons within the apostolic succession, ensures that the shape of the Anglican Communion will be the same in all its provinces. In every Anglican church and chapel the Eucharist (a more appropriate term than "Holy Communion", which is *pars pro toto*) is duly celebrated by ministers who have been ordained by bishops standing in the stream of the apostolic succession; moreover admission to the reception of Communion is normally preceded by the sacramental Confirmation imparted by a bishop.[3] The result of these requirements has been to secure a minimum of necessary uniformity in outward shape between the different Churches and provinces, which are so different in churchmanship, language, religious feeling, and cultural background. Without these Catholic and universal liturgical requirements, it is hard to see how the whole Communion, made up of such different components, could have held together. This Catholic status is fortunately still further embodied in the ineradicably sacramental tone and emphasis of the Book of Common Prayer which, in the two original forms prepared by Archbishop Cranmer and published in 1549 and 1552, remains the basis of all the revised Prayer Books now in use in the different Churches and provinces of the Anglican Communion.

2. PRACTICAL UNITY BASED ON THE
CONSCIOUSNESS OF CONTINUITY

While Anglicans in England and elsewhere are deeply conscious of their real and practical unity of spirit or ethos based on their common worship, there is another bond joining those Anglicans who are members of the Church of England. They are also convinced of a practical unity based on the consciousness of the continuity of their church life with that of the pre-Reformation Church of their own country and its past history. They feel themselves at one and in living continuity with the English Christians of Anglo-Saxon and medieval times by virtue not only of holding a common Catholic faith, but also of membership of the same identical Church.[4]

The post-Reformation Church of England had tended to forget this until the leaders of the Oxford Movement reawakened her to it, but she is now acutely conscious of her unbroken continuity in all essentials with the Church of St Augustine of Canterbury, of St Theodore, of St Dunstan, of St Swithun, of Edward the Confessor, of Archbishops Anselm, Thomas à Becket, and Stephen Langton. A glance at the normal Lectionary of the Church of England of today will reveal the considerable number of pre-Reformation English saints who are commemorated in the course of the year.

The Roman Catholic Church, however, still continues to deny this institutional or ecclesiastical continuity, in spite of the friendly and understanding tone of the recent Decree of the Second Vatican Council on Ecumenism, *Unitatis redintegratio,* of November 1964. The most that this Second Vatican Council was able to say in favour of the Anglican Communion was in these terms: "The Anglican Communion has a special place among those [communions separated from the Roman See] which continue to retain, in part, Catholic traditions and structure" (No. 13).[5] From the Orthodox side many theologians still have grave doubts as to the validity of the Anglican claim to a historical, dogmatic, and sacramental continuity with the pre-Reformation Church of England.

All this is true, but we must remember that "identity" and "continuity" are ambiguous terms, and what is the same or identical in one respect is not necessarily the same or identical in another respect. Unquestionably the Church of England underwent a revolutionary and somewhat violent change in the Tudor period imposed on her by the Crown and Parliament; and the whole of her subsequent history has been conditioned by this theological and structural revolution. But a revolution—even one which shakes the traditional foundations—does not inevitably destroy the underlying identity of the institution which undergoes it. The Church of England has changed no more, and has probably changed less, than the political institutions of the country and she has never lost her sense of the past. It is not necessary to explain this point further to anyone who knows the spiritual atmosphere of the public worship of the Free Churches of this country, even of the Methodist Church. In these Protestant Churches, there is no vivid awareness during the services of anything in Christian history or tradition that occurred before the century of Luther, Zwingli and Calvin.

Though the official post-Tridentine attitude of the Roman Catholic Church towards the Church of England was that she is schismatic and heretical, no sensible observer can deny that she has got some measure of Catholic continuity. By now many Continental Roman Catholic theologians would willingly concede this, even in their books and public statements. What certainly survived the storm of the English Reformation was a worshipping community of Christians which included until about a century ago, a high proportion of the English people and is governed by bishops who still occupy the historic sees. This Church was, and always is, careful to preserve the episcopal succession through the solemn prayers of the Consecration of Bishops and by the laying-on of hands; thus linking the bishops of today with the hierarchy of medieval England.

The Anglican liturgy is derived from Latin Missals and other service-books of the Western Catholic Church of the Middle Ages (in particular the Sarum Missal) by means of translation, paraphrase, abbreviation, and serious omission. Cranmer's First Prayer-Book (1549) retained a markedly Catholic imprint, but, in spite of his conservative cast of mind, he did not hesitate to make, or to permit others to make, many omissions and additions in his Second Prayer Book (1552) in accordance with his own Protestant theological convictions. Yet to this day Anglicans use the same sacraments and the same rites as were used in medieval England, except that the private confession of sins and the anointing of the sick are not widely used.

On the other hand, all Anglicans, not excluding the Evangelicals, believe themselves to be carrying on the tradition of the apostolic faith of the Catholic Church, purged only of certain Roman or papal errors which they judge to be dangerous doctrinal deviations, as for instance, certain Tridentine and Marian dogmas and the papal dogmas of the First Vatican Council. Ever since Cranmer's time, Anglicans have shown, and still show, a persistent tendency to defend their peculiar non-Roman dogmatic position by an appeal to Christian antiquity and to the Fathers; this appeal brings them on to a common ground with the Orthodox Church. It is worth mentioning that in the present-day Roman Catholic Church, patristic studies are flourishing.

5

The continuation of the episcopal hierarchy on which so much depended was made possible by the prudent policy of successive Tudor sovereigns when, by royal command, they imposed their English Reformation on the medieval Church, and co-operated with the bishops, once the latter had accepted the Royal Supremacy and the Elizabethan Settlement. For political as well as religious reasons, the Tudor rulers did not destroy the historic English episcopate. To this co-operation is due the fact that, though the Church of England was at that time so Erastian and so Puritan, she emerged from the Reformation happily uncommitted to any precise or clear-cut new theological system. It was indeed most fortunate that the Church of England was not dominated during the sixteenth century by any theological master-mind such as Luther, Zwingli, or Calvin. No single theologian of genius has ever so dominated her, as to give his name to her, or to impose upon her his peculiar system.

The man who came nearest to doing so was Archbishop Thomas Cranmer, since he gave to her what became the traditional English liturgy, and shaped the forms of Anglican worship which have been in use until the present time. Cranmer's Second and more Protestant Prayer Book (1552) has made a far greater impression on the Church of England than any other official document of the Reformation period, the Thirty-nine Articles included, and every English Anglican has felt it. In any case, Cranmer was an outstanding liturgist with an almost infallible sense for noble prose, but he was not a great systematic theologian. Happily we are not tied to his heretical doctrine of the Eucharist.

The most influential Anglican theoretical writer of the Reformation period was Richard Hooker (1554-1600), but he was not so much the creator of a theological system as the interpreter and defender of what was, by his time, an established fact, namely the way of life into which the Church of England had settled down under Elizabeth I. In his *Treatise on the Laws of Ecclesiastical Polity,* he revealed himself as one of the greatest theologians whom the English Church has ever possessed, and he conveyed his beliefs in a masterly English prose. But, influential though he was and continues to be, the Church of England has never committed herself to his views, especially in matters of episcopacy and Eucharist. We are not the Cranmerian or the Hookerian Church but the Church of England.

3. PRACTICAL UNITY BASED ON A PARTICULAR COMPROMISE

Some people like to describe the Church of England as "the Anglo-Saxon compromise in ecclesiastial matters". They think of this definition as applicable not only to the Elizabethan Settlement but also to the English Church of our time. In a sociological context the expression "Anglo-Saxon compromise" is of course a phrase which comes spontaneously to the mind of everybody, but more markedly to the mind of an observer who comes from the Continent of Europe and has not had the advantage of being born and bred in England. After all, it is notorious that every Englishman in his daily life is continually practising the delicate art of compromise with dexterity and success: much of the political genius of English statesmen is believed to consist in their subtle handling of affairs, so as to attain a sensible compromise. Have not Anglicans, in England and elsewhere, themselves frequently and proudly described their way of Christian life and faith as a *via media*? And what is this *via media* but a happy and prudent compromise between two or more conflicting parties or conflicting theological systems?

But in what actually does a compromise consist? In the proper sense of the word, it is an amicable arrangement or agreement, whereby two or more conflicting parties reach a practical *modus vivendi* by mutual concessions. And this leads to the concrete question: If the present happy co-existence of different theological traditions and tendencies within the Anglican Church is based on some peculiar "compromise" of this kind, what mutual concessions have been made by the different parties to bring it about?

We can be sure of one matter. A compromise of this kind can never be based on sacrifice or concession of any theological principle or important doctrine, such as are still being vigorously pressed by the different schools of thought. The Catholic and Evangelical "parties", especially the Conservative Evangelicals, do not refrain from holding, teaching, or preaching those theological doctrines which appear to them to be true, whatever may be their regard for the theological opinions of the others. They make no effort to hide or play down those convictions and doctrines which are characteristic of their own churchmanship; it would be scandalous and cowardly if they were to do so.

In fact, there is no attempt at a compromise of what the "parties" consider to be essential; compromise only extends to the outward forms in which such theological essentials are expressed, whether they

61

be written formulae or external actions. In other words, the extent of the compromise only covers such matters as the actual wording of official church documents, the careful selection of sometimes vague and ambiguous language, and the use or non-use of certain devotional observances which are not essential, and which might be offensive to other members of the Church.

The 1662 Prayer Book reproduces with very few alterations the 1552 Book which was undoubtedly compiled from a Protestant point of view; yet it is far from being a Protestant manifesto. Protestant words and phrases show what was in the minds of the men who drew up Cranmer's Second Book, but they do not compel the reader or the user of the rite to adopt completely Cranmer's eucharistic theology or the Protestant views of the other compilers.

The same is true of the Thirty-nine Articles of Religion. The Church of England has given general assent to them for so long, that she cannot disclaim all responsibility for their contents. Nevertheless it is true that they were drawn up as a kind of *henoticon* or document to ensure peace and union among the Christians of England during the sixteenth century, but not to provide the national Church with a systematic declaration of faith. They are not a *confessio Anglicana* comparable with the Confessions of the Reformed churches of the Continent. Their assertions therefore tend to be limited, and their statements to be qualified, so as to leave loopholes for the expression of theological points of view which differ from the mild and rather high Calvinism that mainly underlies this document. Considering that it was drawn up in the sixteenth century, the Anglican formulary of the Thirty-nine Articles is indeed a truly comprehensive formulary.

In short, the 1662 Prayer Book and the Thirty-nine Articles were deliberately worded so that Catholics and Protestants alike could interpret them in their own way, and this deliberate ambiguity has been the sole means by which it has been possible up to the present time, for the Church of England to live in her condition of peaceful *symbiosis*, or even to have attained that condition.

Similarly, the occasional efforts which have been made by the episcopal authorities to regulate or forbid certain devotional practices and usages, such as the reservation of the Blessed Sacrament and the extra-liturgical services connected with it, show the same spirit of compromise. The service known as Benediction of the most Holy Sacrament is a peculiar instance.

On the other hand, the well-known additions and insertions which the Anglo-Catholic priests have made to the eucharistic rite of 1662 are felt to lie within the compass of the Anglican compromise. This Protestant composition revised in 1662 was improved by a few judicious insertions (the Propers taken from the Sarum Missal) and by addition of appropriate ceremonial.

This particular compromise does indeed explain how the Church of England has held, and continues to hold, together. At the same time it explains how there must be limits to Anglican unity (comprehensive though it is) at both ends of the spectrum, and not only in England but throughout the Anglican Communion. There are indeed large bodies of devout Christian people who neither can find, nor desire, any place in such a Church as the Church of England.

4. PRACTICAL UNITY WITH SPIRITUAL FREEDOM

It has been pointed out many times that the Church of England and the whole Anglican Communion share many things in common with the Roman Catholic and the Orthodox Churches. These are, among others, the threefold ministry of bishops, priests and deacons, the apostolic succession, the necessity of Confirmation as a normal preliminary to receiving Holy Communion,[6] and a high esteem and reverence for the sacraments of the Catholic Church.

But there is one respect in which the Anglican spirit or ethos (as exemplified in the various versions and revisions of the Book of Common Prayer, and enshrined in four centuries of history) differs most strongly from these two other Catholic Churches; this is the tremendous emphasis which Anglicanism puts on the spiritual freedom of the individual believer. Throughout the whole range of Anglican public worship and Christian life, the permissive *you may* (or the weak *you should*) are found far more often than the mandatory *you must*. This emphasis on spiritual freedom has coloured the whole ethos and expression of Anglicanism. There is no other Church in the Catholic tradition—certainly not the authoritarian Roman Catholic Church as she was before the Second Vatican Council—which so passionately believes in spiritual freedom, and which so positively demands it from clergy and laity alike. (One instance is the Anglican position concerning the vexed question of birth control.) The Anglican version of Catholic Christianity proclaims aloud and with deep conviction the importance of this spiritual, Christian, and responsible freedom. There is no other practical thing of which the Anglican Communion is more entirely convinced, or which it practises so completely.

As a result no priest in all Christendom is as free as an Anglican priest. His spiritual freedom is nearly absolute; it is safeguarded at every turn and point, and, even today, he is more free from interference than a member of any other profession in the modern world.

On the other hand, members of the Church of England and the rest of the Anglican Communion are not unaware of the real danger of this spiritual freedom. If it is true that Anglicanism does believe that the best work is done and the best lives are lived when clergy and laity are trusted with freedom, it is also true that it faces squarely the fact that many will abuse this spiritual freedom. It faces also the fact that, in consequence, some scandals, many anomalies, oddities, and inconsistencies, and much wastage must occur, and that they mar the public image of the Church. Anglicans know very well that their Church, in its present form, carries a high proportion of spiritual passengers whose Christian witness is weak, but the Anglican belief in spiritual freedom is so deep and fundamental that the Anglican Church deliberately rates these considerable dangers as less than the gain which comes from it.

The whole desire of the Church [wrote William Temple] has been to offer the fullness of God's help to every soul, but never to dictate to any soul precisely how that soul may best receive the benefit. It sets a high standard for the individual member. No doubt it involves comparative failure for very many who might, by a more and more military discipline, have been led to a fuller use of the means of grace than in fact they practise under the Anglican system. None the less I believe the Church of England did deliberately adopt this attitude, and I believe it did so rightly. For with all the dangers—in fact, humanly speaking, with all the certain loss involved—there is made possible in this way for all the members of the Church a fullness of individual apprehension and appropriation, which is almost impossible, and is certainly discouraged under a system which marks out for men quite clearly their religious duties so that when they have performed these, they feel that their duty is done.[7]

5. THE ANGLICAN EXPERIMENT

The final result of the unceasing interactions between the three movements in the post-Reformation Church of England—Evangelicalism, Catholicism, and Liberalism—has been that Anglicanism now presents something new in Christianity, a unique combination of Catholic and Protestant (or Evangelical) traditions. The modern Anglican Communion differs from the Church of England of the sixteenth century in theological character quite as much as in its size and organization.

As far as the Church of England is concerned, she emerged from the Reformation as a Church in which a mild and rather tolerant Calvinistic Protestantism predominated, but which allowed a higher proportion of Catholic and liberal elements and insights than was usual in the more rigid Protestant Churches of the Continent. In the sixteenth century, she was in all the theological essentials on the Protestant side. Gradually and increasingly she was led into a theological position *sui generis* in which the two great traditions, one recognizably Catholic, and the other recognizably Protestant or Evangelical, manage to live together in one body, and—which is of supreme importance —in ever increasing harmony and friendliness.

This is the Anglican experiment of peaceful co-existence, and it is now practised to some extent in every Church of the Anglican Communion. It is a modern development, and it is perhaps too early to applaud its final success. Only of recent years has it been widely recognized that such an experiment is being made, and that it ought to be made. Recognition of its necessity has in the past few years become a major factor in preserving the bond of unity within the Church of England, as well as throughout the Anglican Communion at large.

This modern Anglican experiment in amicable co-existence will succeed, provided (and this is a *conditio sine qua non*) that all, or almost all, the leaders in the Church of England accept it, and continue to accept it, as something that is right and desirable on its own merits. Certainly in recent years, especially with the spread of the ecumenical spirit, there has been a growing tendency in the Church of England to regard it as right and desirable. Happily there is an increasing number of responsible leaders of both schools of thought who definitely reject the old partisan policy of trying to seize control of the whole Church and to exclude the other "party" from office and influence. On the other hand, these responsible leaders equally refuse to regard their theological differences as futile or as unimportant.

Many responsible theologians of the Church of England, Catholic as well as Evangelical, are now making a growing effort to enable the Church to hold the two main traditions in tension, not merely as the two complementary sides of one truth, but as traditions which, though at certain points in open conflict, yet must be held simultaneously, if we are all to be led towards a honest resolution of the conflict and to a fuller integration of our comprehension of the Christian truth. Meanwhile, this modern Anglican experiment is being made and goes on. While it is too early to express a definite and objective judgement upon it, it is none the less a highly significant factor which cannot but influence our judgement on such general questions as the possibility of the theological synthesis between the Catholic and the Protestant or Evangelical traditions in one particular Church, namely the Church of England.[8]

5

The Catholic Faith

1. THE FUNDAMENTAL DISTINCTION
BETWEEN FAITH AND THEOLOGY

Before discussing the question of an Anglican theological synthesis between what is true and vital in historic Catholicism, and what is true and vital in historic Protestantism, it is necessary to establish the fundamental distinction, too often overlooked, between faith and theology, and especially between faith and theological opinion, theory, or system. In general terms the real church unity (whether of the universal Church or of some national Church) is unity of faith, order, and sacramental worship and not of theological system. It is increasingly recognized by theologians of many schools that classical Lutheranism and Calvinism as theological systems were very close to the scholastic systems of the medieval and Counter-Reformation periods. In both cases, the leaders failed to distinguish properly the deeper matters of faith from those doctrines which were on a plane of mere theological reflection and systematization.

In Christendom the study of theology is necessary but of secondary importance; but faith given by God is vital, primary, and essential. During and after the Reformation, religious controversy was conducted in an extremely bitter temper and culminated in the Wars of Religion. This may be partly explained by the failure of the theologians on both sides to distinguish clearly between those matters which formed part of the deposit of the divine faith, and those which were merely part of a system of theology devised by men who were too often fallible. But it is not easy to draw a sharp line between those beliefs which make up the substance or reality of faith, and all those human reasonings, deductions, syllogisms, and rationalizations which comprise theology. Even a document such as the Thirty-nine Articles of Religion, which for its time was comprehensive and relatively moderate, shows, in Articles 8-39, an inextricable mingling and apparent confusion of the Catholic faith and of diluted Calvinistic theology.

In this context I use the word "faith" in a quite objective sense; the word refers to the body of truths (the Christian faith), which is to be found, above all, in God's revelation contained in the Bible, and, to a secondary degree, in the creeds of the Church, the dogmatic definitions of recognized General Councils, and in the whole witness, teaching, tradition, and experience of the Catholic Church throughout the ages. The Church holds that this complex doctrine embodies the teachings of Christ himself and of his apostles, or at least follows directly from them. Because it is God's supreme revelation to mankind in Christ and in the power of the Holy Spirit, no man can wilfully reject the substance or reality of the Catholic or orthodox faith, except at the peril of his own salvation.

In contrast, Christian theology exists at a different level; it is a human science and the scientific elaboration of those divinely revealed religious truths which make up the objective faith. Its theme is the being and the nature of God and his creatures, and the whole complex of the divine dispensation from the fall of Adam to the redemption through Jesus Christ, and its mediation to men by Christ's Church, including all those so-called natural truths about God, the soul, moral law, and the like, which are accessible to mere reason. Its purpose is the scientific investigation of the contents of the Christian and Catholic faith by the use of reason, enlightened by divine faith (*fides quaerens intellectum*), so as to be able to understand it more deeply. In the course of time theology has developed a number of specialized branches such as dogmatic, biblical, historical, moral, ecumenical, and pastoral theology. It strives to collect and verify the facts, to sift and compare them, to classify them and discover their mutual relations, to find a language in which to express them as clearly as possible, and to set them out as parts of one coherent and rational system. One more thing is necessary: a professional Christian theologian cannot carry out his task, unless he is a living member of Christ's body, a committed Christian who combines prayer with the employment of his rational faculties.

I. THE DISTINCTION BETWEEN OBJECTIVE FAITH AND ITS FORMULARIES

Another fundamental distinction, also too often neglected or ignored, is that between the objective faith and its formularies. We see from the New Testament that even in the earliest times, there was a single faith accepted by all but formulated in differing ways. The four Evangelists recorded the gospel in very different ways. They designated the one Lord Jesus by different names and adjectives, expressive either of the sublimity or the lowliness of his divine-human person; the one form of words by which the Eucharist was instituted has been transmitted in a variety of ways; the facts of Jesus Christ's passion, death, and resurrection are not recorded in one fixed formula by the early Christians, but in many different testimonies. It is thus quite understandable that, owing to its historical character, the Christian faith has been, and will continue to be, expressed in constantly changing formularies and, we may pray, in less one-sided pronouncements.

In the first four centuries of the Christian era, different Churches and communities used widely varying formularies of the "symbol of faith" in Baptism, which were yet mutually recognized; only from the fourth century onwards were attempts made to have one standard "symbol" for the whole Church. Even then, Christians remained convinced that the Christian faith in all its fullness could not be fully contained by any single formula or Creed—even by that framed by the Council of Nicaea in A.D. 325—and that a difference in formulary must not necessarily be regarded as a difference in faith.

Studying the growth of Christian dogma historically we see that the content of the objective faith (considered as the gift of the Word of God or of the Divine Revelation) is not identical with any particular and historical formulation of it. Many examples can be given. In Christology, for instance, whether the unity of Jesus Christ may be said to be based either on the divine person or on the one divine nature; or in the doctrine of justification, whether justification is through faith alone; or in the doctrine of the Eucharist, whether the consecrated bread and wine remain as bread and wine or whether they do not so remain—and so on.

We are fully justified in drawing this clear distinction between the immutable content or reality of faith, and its formularies—which are always changing, relative, historically-conditioned, and capable of improvement. The Catholic faith is God's gift and remains unchangeable; its formularies, including even the most solemn pronouncements by the Church in the exercise of her teaching office, are by their nature very different and are sometimes apparently contradictory.

In recent years Roman Catholic theologians have shown a far more open recognition of the partial, incomplete, and historically-conditioned character of the solemn declarations of Ecumenical Councils.[1] The necessity of such a new position towards council statements is easily seen, when we are dealing with polemically-oriented and limited statements and canons ending with anathemas, as those of the Council of Trent on the sacraments. However, even the most balanced conciliar definitions, in spite of the efforts of the Fathers to present a well-rounded expression of the Catholic faith, suffer from inevitable limitations. Whenever the reality of the Christian faith is expressed in *propositional* statements from a given time in the *past*, the conciliar formulas (and also the papal formulas in the Encyclicals) are by their very nature provisional and perfectible, in spite of the most exhaustive efforts of their authors to make them complete and adequate for all times.

Through the contemporary dialogue and shared Christian life, Roman Catholics, as well as Anglicans and Protestants, are being compelled in increasing numbers to address their attention more directly to the *pre-propositional* realities which lie behind their necessary but provisional confessional statements (dogmas) and church order. There is a more conscious effort to distinguish between the level of faith which is primary, and the level of confessional statements (dogmas) which are necessary but provisional; between the reality of Christ's Church which is also primary, and church order which is also necessary but still provisional. To put it another way, there is a return to a less *propositional* understanding of the basic reality of faith and revelation, that may well enable the Christian theologians of different Churches to find a solution acceptable to all the great Christian Communions. This would never be possible, if we failed to sound and to probe below the classical formulas and patterns in which the belief and life of the Catholic Church were expressed. All the formulas of faith, even the most solemn definitions, proclaimed by the teaching office of the Church, are imperfect, inadequate, one-sided, historically-conditioned, and provisional. They must constantly be reshaped and reformulated out of the fresh experience of the life of faith in the Church of here and now.

This fundamental distinction was precisely what Pope John XXIII was thinking about, when he said on the opening day of the Second Vatican Council that "the substance of the ancient doctrine of the deposit of faith is one thing, and the way in which it is presented is another".

II. THE SPIRIT OF MUTUAL CHARITY
IN THE CHURCH OF ENGLAND

Before discussing further the problem of a strong unity in the Church of England rooted in Catholic faith, we must consider how the theologians of this Church regard their different dogmatic emphases and their theological disagreements. Do they cultivate the art of listening to one another with charity, attention, and humility, so as to learn from each other in common dependence on the Holy Spirit?

In fact, although controversy in theological matters is brisk and uninhibited (for instance, the diverse and impassioned reactions to *Honest to God* in 1963 and 1964), there is in the contemporary English Church a marked decrease in partisanship and acrimony and, further, a genuine desire for better mutual understanding. Even since the beginning of this century, Anglicans all over the world have played a part in the Ecumenical Movement out of all proportion to their numbers, because the Anglican Communion, of which the Church of England is the mother and the head, is in itself an Ecumenical Movement in miniature.

The Anglican way of life and the institutional unity which is secured by it is, I believe, unique, and its dogmatic and theological bases are being increasingly understood. Such practical and institutional unity, founded on friendly co-existence or *symbiosis*, can be defended on dogmatic and theological grounds only if this pragmatic unity in living, working, and worshipping together is used as an opportunity for all the Anglican traditions to grow together, with increasing mutual regard and affection, a stronger sense of their common inheritance in the Catholic faith, and a progressive agreement on the main theological principles. Diversity is good, if it develops within the faith and is marked by Christian love and tolerance. It enriches the Church, so long as the various traditions of theological thought, and the different liturgical and devotional practices are recognized as being mutually complementary.

It is my conviction that this spirit of charity, this readiness to have a genuine dialogue with others, and to learn from others, is a phenomenon plainly to be seen in the Church of England today. It is also my conviction that, without the fulfilment of these conditions, we could not have arrived at the present vivid awareness of our underlying and deep unity in the Christian and Catholic faith.

I do not think that the Christian and Catholic faith can be maintained (or recovered, if it has been shaken), except within a Church which has outward institutional unity, as the Church of England undoubtedly has. The Church of England is an institutional expression of the spirit of Christian charity and of readiness to learn from others. She does not presume to judge—far less to condemn—other Christian Churches or communities which differ from her; she prizes so highly charity and the willingness to join in discussions with other Churches, that she may rightly claim to have her distinctive contribution to make to the reconciliation of the separated Churches within our divided Christendom.[2]

2. THE TRINITARIAN AND CHRISTOLOGICAL FAITH

I. THE TWO ECUMENICAL CREEDS

The basic elements of the Catholic faith held by the universal Church, and consequently by the Church of England, is succinctly stated in the two great Catholic or ecumenical creeds of the Church, the so-called "Apostles' Creed" or the Western Creed, and the so-called "Nicene Creed" or the Niceno-Constantinopolitan Creed (381). These two creeds possess an ecumenical and Catholic authority which the so-called Athanasian Creed (never formally accepted by the Orthodox Church of the East) lacks. If it be objected that the Apostles' Creed is technically not fully ecumenical on the ground that it is typically Western, it may nevertheless be considered as ecumenical, because all but two of its clauses are included in the Nicene Creed.[3]

A creed may be defined as a concise and formal statement of important points or articles of the Christian and Catholic faith, which has received the sanction of ecclesiastical authority. Originally, in the course of the act of Baptism by triple immersion, a series of short dogmatic questions were addressed to the candidate or catechumen, to each of which he answered, "I believe". The formulas of these questions varied in detail from place to place, but, by the fourth century, they had become more uniform and were everywhere tripartite in structure, following Matthew 28. 19.

Evenually the only creeds that remained in use for this purpose were the Apostles' Creed in the West, and the Nicene Creed in the East. The Council of Nicaea (325) put one of these professions of faith into credal form and promulgated it as a general standard of orthodox belief; then the use of creeds for this second purpose (the test of the orthodox faith) spread rapidly during the fourth century. But there is no evidence to suggest that before the rise of the Arian controversy, the local creeds were formulated, revised, or supplemented with a view to excluding heresy; their purpose was to state positively the fundamental elements of the Christian faith for those who were, in Baptism, entering on the Christian life and fellowship.

We can distinguish two main types of creeds, the Eastern and the Western, and the differences between them correspond in large measure to the differences between the Eastern and the Western mind.

The Western mind was always more practical and more interested in facts than in ideas; the Eastern mind was more speculative and interested in ideas rather than facts. The Western mind was not generally able to speculate for itself, and was not willing to pay much attention to the speculation propounded by Eastern theologians; it opposed error less from the love of truth in the abstract than from motives of practical and moral Christianity and from the wish to be free from the confusion and distractions of theological controversy. Against this, the Eastern mind delighted to think out the intellectual content of the faith and to devote itself to the study of theology; it thus inevitably produced a whole crop of heresies of its aown.

These intellectual characteristics are reflected in the latter development of the creeds of the East. While the Western creeds are mostly short and straightforward recitals of soteriological facts, the Eastern creeds add dogmatic explanations and interpretations. The Western creeds on the whole remain closer to the original purpose of creeds, which was a positive statement of truth, and especially of the primitive *kerygma* or proclamation about the Saviour. The Eastern creeds necessarily show a more obvious desire to define truth and exclude heresy and error; they put the drama of human salvation in its cosmic perspective.

These tendencies can easily be illustrated from the Apostles' and the Nicene Creeds. The former recounts the bare fact of the birth of Jesus Christ; the latter adds that it was "for us men and for our salvation". The former records the fact of the Resurrection on the third day; the latter adds that it was "according to the Scriptures". The Nicene Creed explains that Baptism is "for the remission of sins", and alone has the phrase that "he shall come again with glory". Likewise the Eastern creeds tend to greater dogmatic precision, especially to dwell on the life and status of the Son of God before his incarnation. In the Constantinopolitan Creed (381), as in the earlier form defined at the Council of Nicaea in 325, many clauses stressed his pre-cosmic divinity, especially the famous clause "being of one substance (or essence) with the Father".

The only phrases found exclusively in many Western creeds (but not in all of them) are: "he descended into hell", and "the communion of saints".

II. THE APOSTLES' CREED

The so-called Apostles' Creed, as we use it, falls into three sections concerned with God the Father, Jesus Christ, and the Holy Spirit; it appears to be based structurally on Matthew 28. 19. It is terse in expression and without theological explanation. Though nearly all its affirmations can be supported by evidence from the New Testament, the formula itself does not date back to apostolic times. The title is first found about 390, and soon afterwards the legend appears that it was a joint composition of the twelve Apostles.[4] Local baptismal confessions in use at Rome and in other Western Churches in the fourth century are in approximately the same form as the present creed, with minor variations, and in fact our Apostles' Creed is, according to many scholars, an enlarged form of the old baptismal creed of the Roman Church.

This "Old Roman Creed" is first found in Greek in a letter written by Marcellus of Ancyra about A.D. 340 to Pope Julius and preserved in the writings of Epiphanius. Marcellus had been accused of a form of Sabellianism; and in order to prove his orthodoxy, he left with the Bishop of Rome a formal statement of his faith. This was the same as the baptismal creed of the Roman Church which we find, sixty years later (*c.* 404), described in the commentary of Rufinus of Aquileia, *Commentarius in Symbolum Apostolorum.* In its earlier form, shorter than that which we use, it runs as follows:

1. I believe in God the Father Almighty.

2. And in Christ Jesus, his only Son, our Lord.
   Who was born of the Holy Spirit and the Virgin Mary,
   Who under Pontius Pilate was crucified and buried,
   On the third day rose again from the dead,
   Ascended to heaven,
   Sits at the right hand of the Father,
   Whence he will come to judge the living and the dead.

3. And in the Holy Spirit,
   The holy Church,
   The remission of sins,
   The resurrection of the flesh.[5]

Comparing the Old Roman Creed with our Apostles' Creed, we find the following additions in the latter: "Maker of heaven and earth"— "Who was conceived" — "Suffered" — "Dead" — "Descended into hell"—"God . . . almighty" (on the right hand of God the Father almighty)—"Catholic"—"The communion of saints"—"The life everlasting". The majority of these additions are found in the Creed used by Niceta or Nicetas, bishop of Remesiana in the Balkan peninsula at the close of the fourth century. His creed contained: "Maker of heaven and earth", "suffered", "dead", "Catholic", "communion of saints" "life everlasting", and we reasonably suppose that these additions were in part due to Eastern influences.

The early Latin form of this "Apostolic" Creed may be found in an eighth-century treatise of the Abbot Priminius. Here is a translation of the received text, which reads *sedet* instead of the earlier *sedit*.

I believe in God the Father almighty, creator of heaven and earth;

And in Jesus Christ, his only Son, our Lord, who was conceived by the Holy Spirit, suffered under Pontius Pilate, born from the Virgin Mary, was crucified, dead and buried; he descended into hell; on the third day, rose again from the dead, ascended to heaven, sits on the right hand of God the Father almighty, thence he will come to judge the living and the dead;

I believe in the Holy Spirit, the holy Catholic Church, the communion of saints, the remission of sins, the resurrection of the flesh, and eternal life. Amen.[6]

After the Nicene Creed, the Apostles' Creed is the most important statement of faith in Christendom, even though it is only used in the Western Church. Except in Anabaptist circles, its authority was generally recognized at the Reformation; Martin Luther singled it out as one of the three binding summaries of belief, and both Zwingli and Calvin included it among their dogmatic norms. The Church of England has given unusual prominence to it by requiring it to be recited daily at Mattins and Evensong; but it has never been included among the official dogmatic standards of the Eastern Orthodox Church, and therefore does not form part of her worship, though the suspicion with which the East once regarded it has long since disappeared. In 1920 it was put forward by the Lambeth Conference in its "Appeal to all Christian People" as one of the two creeds which together constitute the second of the four foundations on which the visible unity of the Church might be erected.[7]

III. THE NICENE CREED

The name "the Nicene Creed" is currently used to refer to two distinct creeds, both promulgated by ecumenical councils, which must be carefully distinguished. The first (to which the name should properly be given) is that drawn up by the Council of Nicaea in 325; the second, to which the name "Nicene" is generally given by common usage, is that promulgated by the Council of Constantinople in 381. A more correct name for the latter is "the Niceno-Constantinopolitan Creed", or "the Constantinopolitan Creed".

The Council of Nicaea, the first ecumenical council of the Catholic Church, was summoned by the Emperor Constantine the Great in

325 primarily to try to resolve the Arian controversy. As a test and standard of orthodox belief, the Fathers drew up a creed to defend the Catholic faith against the Arians, and they included the decisive word *homoousios,* or "consubstantial", a technical philosophical word which is not found in the Scriptures. For the first time, a creed was drawn up for the use of bishops rather than of catechumens; it was to be a touchstone by which the doctrines of teachers and leaders could be tested for their correctness and orthodoxy. Compared with later conciliar creeds, it is short, and ends with the words: "And in the Holy Spirit", and then follow four anathemas against Arianism. It may have been based on an earlier Creed of Jerusalem, but its ancestry is too uncertain to be discussed within the scope of this book.

This Creed, as promulgated by the bishops assembled at Nicaea, is in translation as follows:

We believe in one God, the Father almighty, maker of all things visible and invisible;

And in one Lord Jesus Christ, the Son of God, begotten from the Father, only-begotten, that is, from the substance of the Father, God from God, Light from Light, true God from true God, begotten not made, of one substance with the Father (*homoousion tō Patri*), through whom all things came into being, things in heaven and things on earth, who, because of us men and because of our salvation, came down and became incarnate, becoming man, suffered and rose again on the third day, ascended to the heavens, and will come to judge the living and the dead.

And in the Holy Spirit.

But as for those who say, "There was when he was not", and "Before being born, he was not", and that "He came into existence out of nothing", or who assert that "The Son of God is of a different hypostasis or substance, is created, or is subject to alteration or change"—these the Catholic Church anathematizes.[8]

This creed decisively condemned and excluded all the Arian doctrines; the two phrases relating to the divine substance meant that the Son of God shared in the very being (or essence) of the Father. The words "begotten, not made" ruled out the Arian assertion that Jesus Christ, the Son of God, was a creature. The inclusion of the four anathemas sharply distinguishes this creed from any baptismal creed, even though it was based on one. Though added at the Council, they were soon regarded as an integral part of the text.[9]

But it is the creed drawn up or proclaimed by the Council of Constantinople in 381 which is described in Article 8 of the Thirty-nine Articles as "the Nicene Creed". This creed, which is the first of the three official creeds of the Church of England, is in regular use in the liturgical worship of the universal Church both of the East and the West.

There are important differences between the creeds promulgated at the Councils of Nicaea and of Constantinople. In the Constantinopolitan Symbol, the section dealing with the person and human life of Jesus Christ is longer; the brief clause "And in the Holy Spirit" of the Creed of Nicaea, is much developed with a statement on the status and work of the Holy Spirit. After this follow the Constantinopolitan assertion of belief in the Catholic Church, in one Baptism, in the resurrection of the dead and in eternal life. On the other hand, the Nicaean anathemas are missing.

The problem of the origin of this Constantinopolitan Creed is still unresolved. I can only refer readers to the full discussion in Dr Kelly's book.[10] He agrees with the traditional view, namely, that the first Council of Constantinople, which was assembled in 381, promulgated and gave its authority to this creed. In proclaiming this symbol of faith as a suitable formulary of the Church's faith, the Council assumed that it was reaffirming the faith of the Council of Nicaea. It was also convinced that this particular and somewhat more developed formulation of the Nicene faith was well adapted to meet the contemporary heresy against the Holy Spirit then prevalent, and which it felt called to refute.[11]

This symbol of faith, promulgated at Constantinople, was publicly read and acclaimed at the third session of the Council of Chalcedon (451), when it was said to be "the Faith of the 150 Fathers"; referring thus to the bishops who formed the Council of Constantinople. Then, on 25 November 451, the symbol was incorporated, along with the creed of the Council of Nicaea, in the dogmatic definition adopted by the council, and this definition was signed by the papal legate and all the bishops present in the presence of the Emperor Marcian.

The text of this Constantinopolitan Creed in English is as follows:

We believe in one God the Father almighty, maker of heaven and earth, of all things visible and invisible;

And in one Lord Jesus Christ, the only-begotten Son of God, begotten from the Father before all ages, Light from Light, true God from true God, begotten, not made, of one substance with the Father (*homoousion tō Patri*), through whom all things came into existence; who because of us men and because of our salvation, came down from heaven, and was incarnate from the Holy Spirit and the Virgin Mary, and became man, and was crucified for us under Pontius Pilate, and suffered and was buried, and rose again on the third day according to the Scriptures, and ascended to heaven, and sits on the right hand of the Father, and will come again with glory to judge living and dead, of whose kingdom there will be no end;

And in the Holy Spirit, the Lord and the life-giver, who proceeds from the Father, who with the Father and the Son is together worshipped and glorified, who spoke through the prophets; in one, holy, catholic, and apostolic Church. We confess one baptism to the remission of sins; we look forward to the resurrection of the dead, and the life of the world to come. Amen.[12]

In the original Greek, as well as in this translation, the *Filioque* clause is missing. The formula *qui ex Patre Filioque procedit,* which expresses the double eternal procession of the Holy Spirit is not used at all by the Eastern Church and is no part of the original Creed. This doctrine of the double eternal procession appears for the first time as a conciliar dogma in the third anathema of the third Council of Toledo in Spain (589); thence the use of the word *Filioque* during the Mass spread to Gaul and Germany. From the end of the eighth century, this interpolation was inserted in the singing of the Creed at the Mass throughout the Frankish Empire. Pope Leo III refused to accede to a request from Charlemagne to include officially the *Filioque* in the Nicene Creed, but the *Filioque* continued to be sung at Mass, and, soon after 1000 the practice had been adopted even at Rome. Meantime, the Eastern Church opposed its use, which was violently denounced by the Patriarch Photius; this Western uncanonical interpolation became the main point of division between East and West.[13]

As it is well-known, Anglican theologians have generally accepted and defended the Augustinian tradition of the double eternal procession of the Holy Spirit *ab utroque* ("Who proceeds from the Father and the Son"). They followed, almost all of them, the statement of Article 5 of the Thirty-nine Articles.

Speaking for myself, I should like to see this controversial clause (*Filioque,* or *and the Son*) quickly disappear from the revised text of the Roman Catholic Mass and of the Anglican Eucharist. I hope very much that everywhere the Constantinopolitan Creed may be sung according to its original wording, without this divisive and uncanonical addition.

The doctrine which is expressed by this one word, *Filioque,* the eternal procession of the Holy Spirit from the Father and the Son, is indeed an important theological doctrine in Western theology, but it is not a Catholic—that is to say, universal—dogma.

Of all the existing creeds, the Constantinopolitan Creed is the only one for which we can claim a full universal acceptance or ecumenicity. Unlike the purely Western Apostles' Creed, it has been accepted as authoritative in East and West alike ever since Chalcedon (451), and, subject only to the important *Filioque* variation, it is still the norm of Christian Faith. In the Eastern Church, it was accepted by every Orthodox Church, and even took the place of the various local creeds which had been used in the course of the baptismal rite.

However, the Nicene Creed, the creed that Christianity knows best, is not the creed used in the baptismal rite. To the modern Christian it is above all the creed of eucharistic worship. From the sixth century onwards, it has been said or sung during the Liturgy as part of the continuous doxology of the faithful, in Greek, Latin, Slavonic, and other languages, Sunday by Sunday, in the Eucharist, in the Divine Liturgy, in the Mass, in the Lord's Supper, in the Holy Communion. Its majestic rhythm, and its definite but simple and straightforward dogma, marked it out to be the creed of Christian worship. Then at the Reformation its binding dogmatic character was reaffirmed, and its use extended, when it was translated into the national languages of the Reformed churches. In England, Article 8 of the Thirty-nine Articles states: "The three Creeds, *Nicene* Creed, *Athanasius's* Creed, and that which is commonly called the *Apostles'* Creed, ought thoroughly to be received and believed: for they may be proved by most certain warrants of holy Scripture".

IV. THE ATHANASIAN CREED

The so-called Athanasian Creed or "The Creed of St Athanasius" or *"Quicunque Vult"*, which is stated to be one of the creeds of the Church of England by the above-mentioned Article 8 of the Thirty-nine Articles, is not strictly speaking a creed at all. It is rather a Western and Latin summary of orthodox faith and theology for instructional purposes. Besides, this profession of Catholic faith has never possessed the same ecumenical authority as the Apostles' Creed or the Constantinopolitan (Nicene) Creed. The Orthodox Church has never accepted it as a recognized standard of faith nor is it recited in any office of the Eastern Church. At best, this Church treats it as a valuable exposition of dogma.

Now we are quite certain that the Athanasian Creed was not composed by Athanasius of Alexandria, that it was written in Latin and not in Greek, and that it shows a close affinity to the writings of the Latin Fathers St Ambrose and St Augustine and also of St Vincent of Lérins. Moreover, it is not a creed on the traditional pattern. It is an impressive profession of Catholic faith and theology, drawn up probably as a form of elementary instruction concerning the Catholic doctrine, and subsequently used as a kind of psalm or dogmatic canticle. It does not conform to the fundamental credal pattern which arose out of the threefold baptismal formula, nor has it been expanded out of any simpler or earlier creed. Its doctrine is based on earlier creeds but not on its outward form.

Its date and authorship are still obscure and a matter of debate among scholars, from G. J. Voss (1577-1649) and D. Waterland (1683-1740) to the patristic scholars of this century, K. Künstle, A. E. Burn, A. Brewer, C. H. Turner, and Dom Germain Morin. I shall follow here the opinion very prudently proposed by J. N. D. Kelly in his recent book, *The Athanasian Creed* (1964).[14]

He established the following facts. The Athanasian Creed depends on the Trinitarian theology of St Augustine, but it is much more directly indebted to St Vincent of Lérins, and was compiled in the sixth century in south Gaul. The final draft was not the work of St Caesarius of Arles, but was probably drawn up in his milieu and quite possibly at his instigation.[15]

This confession of faith falls in three sections: a summary of the faith in the Trinity (vv. 3-27); then a summary of the faith in the incarnation with a list of the important events of the redeeming works of Christ (vv. 30-41); and finally the "minatory" or "damnatory" clauses, at the beginning and the conclusion and between the two long sections (vv. 1-2, 28-9 and 42).

These "damnatory" clauses have shocked many modern Christians and in particular Anglican Latitudinarians, Broad Churchmen, and Modernists. They are primarily a warning of the terrible consequences that for a Christian must follow the rejection of the Catholic Faith. These clauses may in fact be interpreted in a perfectly normal and charitable way, but it must be admitted that the English translation which is printed in the Prayer Book of 1662 is not always accurate, and is harsher than the Latin original.

I cannot give here the full and correct translation in English of this important document. The critical Latin text may be found in a study by C. H. Turner[16], or in Dr Kelly's book, *The Athanasian Creed*, with an English translation.[17] Neither can I give a detailed analysis of this remarkable dogmatic and theological statement.

I shall confine myself to pointing out that the Athanasian Creed is a wonderful rhythmical composition intended, by its frequent and impressive repetitions, to be committed to memory and to be sung or recited, so as to give summary instruction to the people in the Catholic faith, to prevent the lapse of the orthodox into heresy, and to warn ary.

heretics of the seriousness of their errors. Though not strictly polemical and in no way argumentative or technically theological, it obviously owes its origin to some champion of orthodoxy in times of controversy living in southern Gaul in the sixth century. The very phrase *catholica fides* (the Catholic faith) has the same anti-heretical ring as *catholica Ecclesia* (the Catholic Church) in contrast with the unorthodox sects.

Personally I have no scruple in joining with my colleagues at Winchester Cathedral in the recitation of this profession of faith in full (omitting only the two first verses) at Mattins, on these holy days, when its use is permitted in the Church of England of today (Prayer Book of 1928). The only thing which worries me is that this Western confession of faith and theology contains an explicit statement of the Western theological doctrine of the double eternal procession of the Holy Spirit: "the Holy Spirit is from the Father and the Son, not made, not created, nor begotten, but proceeding". This doctrine of the eternal procession of the Holy Spirit *ex Patre Filioque*[18] was indeed explicitly and systematically taught by St Augustine, but it has no ecumenical or universal authority; it is not a Catholic dogma.

V. THE DOGMATIC DEFINITION OF CHALCEDON

The dogmatic definition of the ecumenical Council of Chalcedon in 451, which is of paramount importance in matters of christology, was accepted by the Churches of East and West, with the exception of the Eastern Monophysite Churches. As a solemn statement of the Catholic faith about Jesus Christ, the incarnate Son of God, it is a largely negative document, defining the external limits of the Christian faith in these christological matters. This dogmatic definition reaffirms the previous definitions of Nicaea (325) and Constantinople (381), asserting that their creeds are a sufficient account of the Orthodox faith about the Person of Jesus Christ. But it declares also that the new errors of Nestorius and Eutyches must be formally repudiated. The dogmatic definition of Chalcedon expressly excluded the views of those who deny the title of *Theotokos* (Godbearer) to the Virgin Mary, the mother of Jesus, thereby implying that the humanity of Christ is separable from his divine Person. The statement excluded also the views of those who confuse the divine and human natures of Christ in one nature, and who therefore hold that the divine nature is, by this confusion, passible and changeable.

The dogmatic definition goes on reasserting the orthodoxy of the synodical letters of Cyril of Alexandria to Nestorius and to the Easterns, and also of the Epistle of Pope Leo I to Flavian of Constantin-ople (the famous *Tome of Leo*).

The Fathers of Chalcedon expressly rejected two heretical doctrines: the duality of Sons in Jesus Christ, and the passibility of the Godhead (namely that the Godhead may suffer). They rejected also any mixture or confusion of the two natures in Jesus Christ, the thesis that the human nature in Christ is of a heavenly or any other essence, and the doctrine which holds the existence of the two natures before the incarnation which became one at the incarnation. Finally the dogmatic definition affirmed the existence of one Person of Jesus Christ subsisting in two natures, divine and human, which are united without confusion, without change, without division, without separation. Explaining this crucial formula, the Fathers said that the distinction of the two natures is in no way annulled by their union, but that rather the characteristics of each nature are preserved in the one Person and one *hypostasis* of the Son of God. In other words, these two natures in Christ are not parted or separated in two persons, but they are united in one and the same Son and only-begotten God the Word, the Lord Jesus Christ.[19]

Since the English theologians of the "New Theology" are affirming that the dogmatic definition of Chalcedon is out of date, obsolete, and irrelevant for intelligent Christians of the twentieth century, I quote, in English translation, the central and main part of this definition:

Wherefore, following the Holy Fathers, we all with one voice confess our Lord Jesus one and the same Son, the same perfect in Godhead, the same perfect in manhood, truly God and truly man, the same consisting of a reasonable soul and a body, of one substance with the Father as touching the Godhead, the same of one substance with us as touching the manhood, *like us in all things apart from sin* (Heb. 4. 15); begotten of the Father before the ages as touching the Godhead, the same in the last days, for us and for our salvation, born from the Virgin Mary, the *Theotokos,* as touching the manhood, one and the same Christ, Son, Lord, Only-begotten, to be acknowledged in two natures, without confusion, without change, without division, without separation; the distinction of natures being in no way abolished because of the union, but rather the characteristic property of each nature being preserved, and concurring into one Person and one subsistence (*hypostasis*), not as if Christ were parted or divided into two persons, but one and the same Son and only begotten God, Word, Lord Jesus Christ; even as the Prophets from the beginning spoke concerning him, and our Lord Jesus Christ instructed us, and the Creed of the Fathers was handed down to us.[20]

It seems clear that the purpose of this dogmatic definition was not precisely to make an accurate and final statement of a dogmatic truth, but it was rather to define the limits of legitimate speculation on christological matters, and to rule out theological and heretical speculations which the Fathers considered as destructive of the purity and completeness of the biblical and Catholic Faith.

This dogmatic definition tries to hold together, in a firm equilibrium, the two sides or aspects of the christological dogma. The first aspect is the absolute oneness of Jesus Christ, and the absolute identity of the Person of the God-Man with that of the *Logos* or the eternal Son. The incarnate Son, Jesus Christ, is not parted or divided into two persons or *prosopa*. The second aspect of the christological dogma is that, side by side with this personal unity, the Chalcedon definition teaches the full reality of Christ's human life and the fact that, as incarnate, the Word exists "in two natures", each complete and retaining its distinctive properties and operations unimpaired in the union. The definition singles out the technical words *hypostasis*, along with *prosopon*, to express the oneness of the Person of the Emmanuel (God with us), thereby distinguishing it once and for all from *physis*, which is reserved for the two natures, divine and human, of the incarnate Son of God.

This dogmatic definition of Chalcedon corroborates the validity of the distinction which I have previously made between the Catholic faith and its formulations. It is quite possible to envisage that, later on in a real ecumenical council, the great Catholic Church of the future could propose a new and more accurate definition of the same christological truth and faith, of the same faith of Chalcedon but expressed in another terminology. In this case, namely, in this eventual dogmatic definition, the typical Greek and static words *hypostasis, prosopon,* and *physis* might be replaced by other words more easily understood by Christians of the twenty-first century. The philosophical perspective underlying this new definition might be also less essentialist, less Greek, less scholastic, and more existentialist, more dynamic, more appropriate, and more relevant to our technological age.

3. THE OTHER INDISPENSABLE ARTICLES OF FAITH

There are six other fundamental truths or articles of faith that are not explicitly mentioned in the creeds or in the Chalcedonian definition. They are essential dogmatic doctrines which form part of the Christian and Catholic faith, and are consequently a necessary part of the faith of the present Church of England and eventually of the great Catholic Church of the future.

It is quite possible indeed that the so-called Catholic and Protestant traditions could be brought together to accept and wholeheartedly to proclaim these six dogmatic truths as a further basis of agreement on dogma for the reunited ecumenical Church of the future.

These six fundamental truths of Christian and Catholic faith seem to group themselves into three sets or pairs; the two truths or principles in each set or pair are mutually complementary. These complementary aspects of truth have in the past given rise—and still give rise—to internal and mutual tensions, for it is broadly true that (within and without the Church of England) the so-called Catholic tradition has laid its main emphasis on one aspect of each of these three pairs of complementary truths, while the so-called Protestant or Evangelical tradition has stressed the other. Always there has been a danger for each tradition to ignore or undervalue the truths which are emphasized by the other.

No doubt such differing emphases will still continue in the great reunited Church of the future, but they would live on only as legitimate variations of theological emphasis. This ecumenical Church, gathering within her bosom the vast majority of committed Christians, will stand clearly and unequivocally bound to both sides or aspects of dogmatic truth, and this will greatly assist in preventing each remaining tradition from overstressing and perverting any particular aspect of truth. The reunited Church of the future will have to accept and proclaim these six dogmatic truths, in addition to the creeds and the definitions of the early Church, as a summing-up of her basic attitude to the dogmatic issues raised at the time of the Reformation, and to the doctrinal divergences which have since developed.

These six pairs of dogmatic truths or articles of faith are the following. The great reunited Church of the future will, first of all, assert the Pauline dogma of justification by grace through faith alone, complemented by the paramount importance of the sacraments. She will assert the primary and final authority of the Bible, complemented by the secondary but very important authority of the doctrinal Tradition of the Church. Finally she will also assert the spiritual nature of Christ's Church, complemented by the historical and institutional nature of the Church, including the ordained ministry and the historic episcopate.[21]

I. JUSTIFICATION BY FAITH AND SACRAMENTS

All Christians, theologians and believers, whether Roman Catholic, Anglican, Protestant, or Orthodox, should be able to agree that the Pauline teaching on justification by grace through faith alone in Jesus Christ as included and explained at length in the New Testament, is one of the most important and vital truths of the Christian revelation. As a matter of history, the Reformation of the sixteenth century began when Martin Luther rediscovered this Pauline teaching; in it the Reformation Churches then found the key which unlocked for them the meaning of the New Testament. It became the source of their spiritual life and the starting-point of their particular theological development.[22]

But we must begin at the beginning with the Apostle Paul who was at once the fervent herald of the doctrine of the justification of the sinner by grace through faith alone, and the theologian who methodically expounded it. About A.D. 56-7 he wrote his *Letter to the Galatians,* after he had heard that a Jewish counter-mission was requiring his Galatian converts to keep all the commandments of the Jewish law, thereby placing in jeopardy the whole value of their faith in Christ. In his letter, the Apostle proclaims his own message, concisely and in impassioned words.

We ourselves are Jews by birth, not Gentiles and sinners. But we know that no man is ever justified by doing what the law demands, but only through faith in Christ Jesus; so we too have put our faith in Jesus Christ, in order that we might be justified through this faith, and not through deeds dictated by law; for by such deeds Scripture says, *No mortal man shall be justified.* . . .
I have been crucified with Christ: the life I now live is not my life, but the life which Christ lives in me, and my present bodily life is lived by faith in the Son of God, who loved me and sacrificed himself for me. I will not nullify the grace of God; if righteousness comes by law, then Christ died for nothing (Galatians 2. 15-21, N.E.B.).

Justification by grace through faith alone is the main theme of the first five chapters of the Epistle to the Romans, the longest and most systematic of all St Paul's letters, which he wrote at Corinth, probably about A.D. 58.

In the third chapter we find one of his most vital texts on the subject of justification by grace through faith.

But now, quite independently of law, God's justice has been brought to light. The Law and the prophets both bear witness to it: it is God's way of righting wrong, effective through faith in Christ for all who have such faith—all, without distinction. For all alike have sinned, and are deprived

85

of the divine splendour, and all are justified by God's free grace alone, through his act of liberation in the person of Christ Jesus. For God designed him to be the means of expiating sin by his sacrificial death, effective through faith. God meant by this to demonstrate his justice, because in his forbearance he had overlooked the sins of the past—to demonstrate his justice now in the present, showing that he is both himself just and justifies any man who puts his faith in Jesus.

What room then is left for human pride? It is excluded. And on what principle? The keeping of the law would not exclude it, but faith does. For our argument is that a man is justified by faith quite apart from success in keeping the law (Romans 3. 21-8, N.E.B.).

Without a doubt, St Paul's teaching of justification by grace through faith alone is a Christian and Catholic dogma, the vital importance of which must be accepted and believed without qualification by every Christian man and woman. This doctrine may be explained as follows: the grace of God, or his free love towards mankind, is extended unconditionally to every man—that is, to every sinner—provided only that this act of divine generosity is accepted by the recipient of his own free-will. The grace of God puts justified sinners into a right personal relationship to himself, through the reconciling work of Jesus Christ. On their part, sinners respond by the act of acceptance, that is, by their trust and confidence in Christ, which replaces their natural urge to justify themselves. In more technical—but always Pauline—language, justification of the sinner is effected by the free gift of the grace of God alone, personally accepted by faith alone; such faith consists in personal trust and loving confidence in the personal God who has revealed himself in Christ.

This doctrine of justification by grace through faith alone, as we find it explained by St Paul in his letters, and also, equally forcibly but in less technical terms, in the Gospels (especially in the parables of God's mercy in Luke, ch. 15), is a central and crucial part of the Gospel message, and so, of course, of our Christian and Catholic faith. The so-called "Catholic" and especially the post-Tridentine theology regarding justification, and equally the so-called "Protestant" or Reformed theology on the same subject, especially its legalistic explanations developed by Luther and the other Reformers, are not in any way on the same level as the plain teaching of St Paul; he was inspired by the Holy Spirit, when he was writing or dictating his canonical letters. Only the dogmatic Pauline truth is necessary; the elaborations of it by theologians may be useful but are often contradictory.

The dogmatic doctrine of justification by grace through faith alone, brought to light in the New Testament and fully rediscovered by the Reformation Fathers, is indeed a fundamental and characteristic dogma of the Christian Church; it is necessary to the Christian doctrine of salvation and to the plenary Faith of the Catholic Church. This Pauline doctrine of justification is a crucial and integral part of the Gospel and of the faith of the universal Church; but the same cannot be claimed for the Lutheran theological system of justification.

Though it contained many theological exaggerations, deficiencies and inaccuracies (in part due to the over-juridical mind), the Reformation doctrine of justification was a new and fresh understanding of a theme which is essentially necessary to the gospel of Jesus Christ. We cannot doubt that it was brought about by the operation of the Holy Spirit himself, working through the Reformers of the sixteenth century.

As a complement to the "Evangelical" or Reformed doctrine of justification by grace through faith alone, the great reunited Church of the future will have to proclaim likewise the paramount importance of the two gospel sacraments, Baptism and the Eucharist or Holy Communion, which were explicitly ordained by Christ as recorded in the Gospels. They are truly means of grace, and generally necessary to salvation. The Ecumenical Church of the future will also have to proclaim the great importance of the other sacraments which are also means of grace. There is no point in discussing here the controversial questions of Penance and the number of these other Sacraments.

All Christian theologians alike—Roman Catholic, Orthodox, Anglican, and Protestant—agree that the universal necessity to salvation of Baptism and the Eucharist is clearly founded on the New Testament texts, that this is taught in all the present Churches, and that it may be considered as a dogma in the wider meaning of that term. This truth must be one of the fundamental doctrines on which the future Ecumenical Church will be explicitly based.

But it is essential to notice the part which the Church, the institutional Church, has to play. The divine act of justification of the sinner through his own faith brings men, women and even children into the body of the Church. In the receiving of the sacraments, God himself offers to men the redeeming power of his Son in ways appropriate to their various needs. The sacraments are thus the normal channels within the Church whereby the divine grace in Christ is brought to mankind. This is the faith of the Church on the sacraments.

Now anticipating the next chapter on theological principles, I should like to set out some general principles of Christian theology on this subject which would appear to follow directly from this dogmatic truth and from church experience. I put them down to present this article of faith in its proper perspective, and to connect it with the spiritual experience of the Church through the centuries.

(i) In each sacrament God himself is active, bestowing his grace in Christ by means of external signs.

(ii) All sacramental rites derive their virtue from the activity in them of Christ who, through the Holy Spirit, continues the work begun in the days of his earthly ministry.

(iii) That work is always redemptive, and the sacraments are means whereby the benefits of Christ's passion are applied to the needs of sinful men and women.

(iv) Christ now acts in the world through his Body, the Church. The sacraments belong to the Church, being part of her corporate life, and having their meaning within that corporate life. The sacraments are social and corporate rites of the Church in which, by the means of divinely appointed signs, spiritual life flows from God.

(v) In Christian theology, the bestowal of grace by means of the sacraments has been held to rest upon divine appointment, which thus supplies the basis of assurance to the worshipper. This appointment may have been effected in a variety of ways, and need not be restricted to explicit institution by Jesus Christ himself. It can also be found in the action of the Apostolic Church, taken under his authority and guided by his Spirit. This statement does not agree with the narrow and restrictive "Protestant" view of those sacraments which are not the "Gospel sacraments".

(vi) There is a clear distinction between the sacraments and magic. In magic the use of the correct formula is believed to enable the wizard to control extra-human powers, but the Christian belief in the efficacy of the sacraments is founded in the faith of the worshipper that, according to the New Testament, God bestows his gifts of grace through certain appointed signs.

(vii) The sacraments are rightly called "effectual signs". As signs, they represent the gifts of grace offered through them; as effectual signs they are means or instruments whereby God confers those gifts on worshippers who receive them with faith.[23]

I wish to add that in a true Christian life no human merit can secure salvation, since there is always implied a need for personal response of acceptance of the divine grace and for self-commitment to God in Christ through loving faith and trust.

On the other hand, this inward response of the justified sinner cannot be separated from outwards participation in the sacraments. Indeed this response, made in faith and through faith, cannot be a transaction between God and the individual soul, effected without reference to the Church, for it is precisely through the sacraments that justification brings men and women into that Body. In other words, the fact and the doctrine of justification by faith alone cannot be separated from the Church and from the sacraments, either in theory or in practice.

II. HOLY SCRIPTURE AND THE DOCTRINAL TRADITION OF THE CHURCH

A second pair of complementary truths which the great reunited Church of the future will jointly assert is, on the one hand, the sovereignty and final authority of the Bible as the primary and ultimate standard of Christian faith and morality, and on the other hand, as a secondary authority, the doctrinal Tradition of the Church as the witness, the safeguard, and the interpreter of biblical faith and morality.[24]

If there is to be a progress towards the peaceful resolution of the conflict between the Catholic and Protestant theological doctrines, the now-divided Churches will have to recognize officially that the Bible which they venerate as holy Scripture is their ultimate and decisive standard of faith and morality. This is surely a *conditio sine qua non* of any future ecumenical reunion in one Church, and its acceptance is as inescapable as that of the dogma of justification by grace through faith alone.

As a matter of fact, the Bible being a collection of books which go deeply into both religious and secular subjects, must be highly honoured by all Christians, on the ground that it is the classical statement of the progressive self-revelation of God in history, culminating in Jesus Christ; it is the authoritative record of God's activity, teaching and saving mankind. Above all, it is the primary sovereign and sufficient criterion of the faith and morality of the Church and her chief source of guidance for her spiritual life.

The Church has accepted this particular collection of books as canonical Scripture, and this fact invests the Bible as a whole, both the Old Testament and the New Testament, with an authoritative character binding on all her members. In particular in the New

Testament there was crystallized, under the guidance of the Holy Spirit, the essential teaching which the Apostles themselves gave to the Church. They were enabled to declare the Gospel through their experience and eye-witness, by the interpreting work of the Holy Spirit on their hearts and minds, and by the direct commission of Jesus Christ. In addition, the New Testament ensures that the historic facts of the revelation given by Christ will be preserved. Thus the Church continues to have a standard to which to refer in matters of faith and morality, from which she may ascertain the authentic gospel, and distinguish between a genuine and growing understanding of the once-given truth, and deviations and distortions of that truth.

On the other hand, the Bible must not be isolated and separated from the Church and her legitimate doctrinal Tradition; the Scriptures cannot be regarded as a kind of ready-made revelation fallen from heaven, or as a sort of quarry full of clear dogmatic propositions. We cannot rightly claim either infallibility or factual inerrancy for the Bible in any crude sense. This matchless Book is really and supremely the Word of the Living God, expressed in human books and through human intermediaries, whose minds are of necessity limited and fallible.

That the Scripture is our supreme and sufficient authority in matters of faith and morals, is a truly Catholic principle which was expressly admitted and practised by the undivided Church of the first millenium, in particular by the Fathers. It was subsequently obscured in the medieval period; but the Reformation brought it again to light, and so gave effect once more to this Catholic dogma.

For Anglicans it is formulated in a moderate and rather negative manner in Article 6 of the Thirty-nine Articles, the first paragraph of which reads:

Holy Scripture containeth all things necessary to salvation so that whatsoever is not read therein, nor may be proved thereby shall not be required of any man, that it should be believed as an article of faith, or be thought requisite or necessary to salvation.

The Bible is today recognized, in the Anglican Communion and in all Protestant Churches, as the final and decisive authority in all matters of faith and morals. The Church acts only as the teacher, the guardian, the defender, and the interpreter of this faith and moral code already expressed in this book.

As for the Roman Catholic Church, a most important official statement was made on this matter, within the last few years, in paragraph

21 of the Dogmatic Constitution on Divine Revelation, approved by the Second Vatican Council and promulgated by Pope Paul VI on 18 November 1965. Here is the first half of this paragraph:

> The Church has always venerated the divine Scriptures, just as she venerates the body of the Lord, since, from the table of both the word of God and of the body of Christ, she unceasingly receives and offers to the faithful the bread of life, especially in the sacred liturgy. She has always regarded the Scriptures, together with sacred Tradition, as the supreme rule of faith, and will ever do so. For, inspired by God and committed once and for all to writing, they impart the word of God himself without change, and make the voice of the Holy Spirit resound in the words of the prophets and apostles. . . . And the force and power in the Word of God is so great that it remains the support and energy of the Church, the strength of faith for her sons, the food of the souls, the pure and perennial source of spiritual life.[25]

At the same time as we accept the supreme authority of Scripture, it cannot be considered in artificial isolation; it must be read and interpreted by the Church, witnessing, safeguarding, and interpreting biblical faith and morality, in accordance with her doctrinal and moral Tradition. This statement complements the "Evangelical" emphasis on Scripture which we have just been considering.

First we should distinguish two different meanings of the word "tradition". It can mean the apostolic Tradition recorded in the books of the New Testament; obviously there cannot be any antithesis between Scripture and Tradition in this sense, for they are identical. But tradition can also mean—and this is the sense which I ascribe to the term "Church Tradition"—the post-apostolic Tradition of doctrine and morals, the Church's growing understanding of the meaning and implications of the apostolic Tradition, and her attempts to preserve it from distortion and corruption. In this sense Tradition includes the ecumenical creeds, the "Rule of Faith", and the *consensus fidelium*, the agreement of the faithful reached under the guidance of the Holy Spirit. Therefore it follows that we can never regard Tradition in this sense as a completed and static body of teaching.

Next we must emphasize the close connection which exists between this Tradition and Holy Scripture. For the Bible is the Word of God recording, especially in the New Testament, the message entrusted to the Apostles by Christ and the Holy Spirit, and consigned to writing under the inspiration of that Spirit. Tradition hands on this Word to the successors of the Apostles. Thus, led by the light of the Spirit, successive generations of church pastors, bishops and priests have faithfully preserved the Word of God in their preaching; they have explained it and made it more widely known. For this reason we must accept and regard both the Scriptures (especially the New Testament) and the post-apostolic doctrinal Tradition with reverence and devotion. Both form part of the whole Tradition of the Church's unique and unchanging life in the truth which is guided and activated by the Holy Spirit.

But, even if the Bible and church doctrinal Tradition are so closely connected, we should nevertheless treat this church Tradition as subordinate and secondary to the supreme authority of the Bible. The main function of this Tradition is to witness, safeguard, defend, and interpret biblical faith and morality, and not to supersede or overrule it.

Is it not possible that the great reunited Church will accept the doctrinal position of the Church of England, and of the Anglican Communion in this matter? It is well-known that Anglicanism does not in any way reject the post-apostolic doctrinal Tradition, or admit the Calvinistic principle of *Sola Scriptura*. It prefers to consider and value this Tradition *after* Scripture and in conformity with it, as a real, very important norm of Christian Faith and morality, though of derivative and secondary value. This Tradition must be recognized as the Church's collective understanding and authoritative interpretation of the divine revelation recorded in Scripture. Because she is united to Jesus Christ her head, and because the Spirit dwells within her, she is steadily growing in her understanding of the truth. Accordingly all her members must hold in deep reverence her collective wisdom and official teaching in matters of faith and morality.

But even this church Tradition, and *a fortiori* all the human traditions of the Church, must be judged by the Bible and be subordinate to it. Every doctrine which is claimed to be part of the Tradition—even one solemnly proclaimed as a dogmatic truth—must be judged and tested by this higher standard. The Church has no right to put forward doctrines which are clearly contrary to Scripture, or which make positive additions to it. It follows that nothing which cannot be proved from Scripture is a necessary part of the Christian faith; if Tradition and the Bible appear to conflict or differ, then the biblical teaching must prevail. Every church tradition, even those affecting doctrine and morals, must be constantly be interpreted, tested, and (if necessary) corrected in the light of the Scripture.[26]

I am sure, for instance, that the great Catholic Church of the future will have to attach a very high degree of authority to the ecumenical creeds of the early Church which have received the assent of the

Catholic Church throughout the ages as witnessing to, safeguarding, and explaining certain fundamental scriptural truths.

III. THE CHURCH AS A MYSTERY AND AS AN INSTITUTION

The third pair of complementary truths which the great reunited Church of the future will surely proclaim, is the double—invisible and visible—aspect of Christ's Church, that is, that she is at once spiritual and institutional. The Church is a personal fellowship and communion with God in Jesus Christ, and, at the same time, she possesses a historical and institutional character summed up in the common acceptance by all the reunited Churches of an ordained ministry, and in particular of the historic ministry of the episcopate.[27]

On the first of this pair of complementary truths, the Mystery of the Church, we can hardly improve on the words of the Dogmatic Constitution on the Church, which was approved by the Second Vatican Council on November 1964. After the publication of this solemn statement *Lumen gentium,* it might appear ungenerous to point out that this aspect of the nature of the Church, as primarily a personal fellowship of men with God and with others in Christ, is a specifically Protestant insight.

Yet, as a matter of history, it was strongly stressed by the Reformers of the sixteenth century. They reacted, somewhat onesidedly, against an over-juridical and institutional conception of the Church and defined her primarily by reference to divine grace and faith, rather than to the social and external continuity of the ecclesiastical hierarchy.

Without doubt the universal Church is, in her deepest sense, the community of the elect or of those who have saving faith in Christ; she is the holy people of God and Christ's mystical Body. Above all else, the Church is a personal fellowship of the redeemed with their heavenly Father in the love of the Holy Spirit; she is also the fellowship of each with the other in Christ, inside and outside the boundaries of the Church. This fellowship comes into being and grows, as they respond in loving faith to the gospel which is presented to them in the holy Scripture and in the sacraments. This spiritual aspect of the Church is a fundamental truth, the recognition of which must be an essential component of the dogmatic basis of any future reunion of the now divided Churches into the great Ecumenical Church of the future.

In chapter 1 of the Dogmatic Constitution on the Church, *Lumen Gentium,* the Second Vatican Council has proclaimed in beautiful and biblical language that the Church is at once spiritual and visible. Paragraph 8 begins with these words:

Christ, the one Mediator, established and ceaselessly sustains here on earth this Holy Church, the community of faith, hope and charity, as a visible structure. Through her he communicates truth and grace to all. But the society furnished with hierarchical agencies and the Mystical Body of Christ are not to be considered as two realities, nor are the visible assembly and the spiritual community, nor the earthly Church and the Church enriched with the heavenly things. Rather they form one interlocked reality which is comprised of a divine and a human element. For this reason, by an excellent analogy, this reality is compared to the mystery of the incarnate Word. Just as the assumed nature inseparably united to the divine Word serves him as a living instrument of salvation, so, in a similar way, does the communal structure of the Church serve Christ's Spirit, who vivifies it by way of building up the body (cf. Ephesians 4. 16).

This is the unique Church of Christ which in the Creed we avow as one, holy, catholic, and apostolic.[28]

I cannot quote here other extracts from the Dogmatic Constitution on the Church.[29] The readers who desire to learn the present official position of the Roman Catholic Church on the spiritual and mystical aspect of the Church, are advised to peruse the chapters i, The Mystery of the Church, and ii, The People of God.

Alongside this primary and spiritual aspect of the Church, the great reunited Church of the future will proclaim as a complementary article of faith, the historical, institutional, and social aspect of Christ's Church. This matter, already made manifest in the New Testament, will be demonstrated in practice by the acceptance, by all the Churches which will come together, of one single ordained ministry, and in particular of the historic and apostolic episcopate.

Every scheme which may be devised for reunion between various separate Churches will have to include a clear recognition of the following truth which has always been emphasized by the "Catholic Tradition". It is that the personal fellowship of men with God and with each other in Christ must be mediated in and through a visible society. All must recognize that Christ's Church is, and always will be, a visible and institutional society, and that everything which gives a visible and social form and effect to the inward and spiritual aspect of the Church, is significant and important.

The inward and mystical unity of the faithful in Christ requires an outward and institutional unity of life and worship. The latter is not only the natural expression of the former, but is, to no small degree, a necessary condition of it. Indeed the outward and liturgical activities of the Church, the preaching of the Word, and the administration of the sacraments and sacred rites, are the basic means by which her inward and spiritual unity in Christ is made secure. Such things may be sufficient to enable all men to recognize the visible Church. And in this context it is worthwhile quoting Article 19 of the Thirty-nine Articles:

The visible Church of Christ is a congregation of faithful men, in the which the pure Word of God is preached, and the Sacraments be duly minis-tered according to Christ's ordinance in all those things that of necessity are requisite to the same.

But the visible and institutional Church ought to be the full expres-sion of the inward and spiritual unity. Preaching and the administra-tion of the sacraments are not of themselves sufficient for this purpose. The visible Church ought to provide the social setting in which the internal and mystical unity of the Christian fellowship in Christ can be fostered and developed to its utmost extent; and so Christ's Church must present a full outward unity of Christian life and order, and a full unity in the essentials of public worship, though with a large diversity in its details. For this there will have to be, in the great reunited Church of the future, one ordained ministry, recognized by all. All the component Churches in the reunited Church will have to accept with a good conscience the ministrations of all ordained minis-ters—deacons, priests or presbyters, and bishops—so that there will be no obstacle to unity in public worship and in the administration of the sacraments.

The Catholic Church is still today disunited. We pray that in the future she will attain complete unity of faith and order, but she is, and will continue to be, a fellowship through time and across space. It is therefore very important that the Church must show her outward continuity from the past, through the present and into the future, as well as her outward unity across the whole world. Continuity in preaching and in the administration of the sacraments is the essential sign of continuity of her unity down the centuries; this is true, but it is not enough. The existence of an ordained ministry based on the principle of historical continuity has had, and will continue to have, a high value in bearing witness to the Church's unity and consolidating it from one generation to another, in the same way as a generally recog-nized ordained ministry bears witness to her unity and consolidates it in every country at any particular time.

With many other theologians, "Protestant" as well as "Catholic", I am convinced of the great value of the historic episcopate in the apostolic succession, and that this ministry should be unanimously accepted by every Church which will form part of the great reunited Church of the future. Supported by the two lesser degrees of the diaconate and the priesthood or presbyterate, it could fulfil, in a unique degree, those two unifying functions in time and place, which I have mentioned. Up to the Reformation, the apostolic episcopate enjoyed almost universal recognition; the reunited Church should again accept this historic principle, and so recover a powerful bond of continuity which cannot be paralleled by any other form of ecclesiastical ministry.

It is clear that in the first century the Church attached great importance to the principle of orderly succession in the ministry, and that in the second century she valued the episcopate, because she believed that she should be based on that principle, which represents a strand of continuity going back to the ministry of the Church in the days of the Apostles themselves. Since the second century this principle of continuity has been clearly preserved in the episcopate by the observance of the rule which restricts the function of ordination and consecration to bishops who have, at their own consecrations by existing bishops, received authority to fulfil this function.

If the present divided Churches are to be reunited, as I fervently hope and pray, into the great Catholic Church of the future, this reunited Church will accept the historic episcopate in the apostolic succession, and she will acquire an ordained ministry which will not only be generally recognized, but will also bear witness to the unity of the Catholic Church both down the centuries and over the whole planet.[30]

Any scheme of reunion will have to include these two complementary truths which are respectively contained in the so-called "Catholic" and "Protestant" understandings of the Church, both the wholehearted acceptance of her essentially spiritual nature (the "Mystery of the Church") and a general acceptance of the historic episcopate. *A fortiori,* these two truths should form a part of the dogmatic basis of the ultimate reunion of the now divided Churches into the great Ecumenical Church at some future time.

In saying this, I do not wish at all to belittle the non-episcopal ministries and all those great Protestant Churches which have, since the Reformation, been served by such a ministry. It is Christ himself who calls and consecrates men to the ecclesiastical ministry, and he is not tied to any particular form or ritual. On the other hand, I am compelled to say that the Roman Catholic "dogmas" of the primacy of supreme jurisdiction of the Roman Pontiff by divine right, and of his infallible teaching *ex cathedra* in some circumstances by virtue of a personal charisma, cannot be regarded as Catholic dogmas. Ever since these papal claims were first made, they have been forcibly denied and rejected by the Eastern Orthodox Church.[31]

The Decree on Ecumenism, *Unitatis Redintegratio* promulgated in 1964 by the Second Vatican Council and Paul VI, is a very promising statement, quite new in the Roman Catholic official teaching, about the notion of an order or hierarchy of truths. It is important, because it asserts that the Roman Catholic Church recognizes that even the dogmas she herself has proclaimed as *de fide* vary in their relationship to the foundation of the Catholic faith. This statement which I quote below is likely to prove most useful in ecumenical conversations with the Roman Catholic theologians.

Furthermore, Catholic theologians engaged in ecumenical dialogue, while standing fast by the teaching of the Church, and searching together with separated brethren into the divine mysteries, should act with love for truth, with charity, and with humility. When comparing doctrines, they should remember that in Catholic teaching there exists an order or "hierarchy" of truths, since they vary in their relationship to the foundation of the Christian faith. Thus the way will be open for this kind of fraternal rivalry to incite all to a deeper realization and a clearer expression of the unfathomable riches of Christ (cf. Ephesians 3. 8).[32]

6

Unity and Diversity in Theology

1. THE DISTINCTION BETWEEN
THEOLOGICAL PRINCIPLES AND
THEOLOGICAL THEORIES AND SYSTEMS

Before we can discuss the theological foundations of Church unity in the compass of the Catholic faith, we must draw a very definite distinction between *theological principles* (or theological fundamental doctrines), and *theological speculations, theories, and systems*.

I understand by *theological principles* these theological fundamental doctrines which are clearly and directly deduced from the manifest doctrinal and moral teaching of the Bible (especially from the New Testament), from the solemn and accepted pronouncements of the undivided Church, and from the undisputed and universal experience of the Catholic Church—always taking into account the growth of human intelligence, moral conscience, and sensibility.

Even though, when stated so baldly, the distinction might seem obvious as that between faith and theology, it is not always easy to draw a clear line between them. But it must be realized, even in the ecumenical climate of the present day, that professional theologians of all Churches are not always sufficiently cautious and careful in their thinking, language, and writing. There are still too many that fall into the temptation of treating theological opinions and speculations as if they were true theological principles. In the past, this confusion has made many of the theological controversies far more bitter and intractable than they need have been.

One concrete example of this crucial distinction, albeit one of the most refractory problems, is that of the nature of the Eucharist.

At the start I state the faith of the Catholic Church, using the prayer of the eucharistic liturgy of the Eastern Orthodox Church. Before the priest and the deacon receive the Holy Mysteries, they say together:

I believe, Lord, and I acknowledge that thou art in truth the Christ, the Son of the living God, which came into the world to save sinners, of whom

I am the chief. I believe also that this is indeed thy most pure Body, and that this is indeed thy precious Blood. Therefore I pray thee: Have mercy upon me, forgive me my offences, voluntary and involuntary; and count me worthy to partake without condemnation of thy most pure mysteries, unto remission of sins and unto everlasting life. Amen.

Another more explicit, but typically Western, expression of the same Catholic faith can be found at the beginning of Article 28 of the Thirty-nine Articles:

The Supper of the Lord is not only a sign of the Love that Christians ought to have among themselves one to another; but rather is a Sacrament of our Redemption by Christ's death: insomuch that to such as rightly, worthily, and with faith, receive the same, the Bread which we break is a partaking of the Body of Christ, and likewise the Cup of Blessing is a partaking of the Blood of Christ.

In these two statements of East and West, we find the Catholic faith regarding the eucharistic sacrament. It was universally accepted from the very beginning that through faith the consecrated bread and wine conveyed to the believers the Body and Blood of Christ. After their consecration, these eucharistic elements were commonly referred to as the Body and Blood of the living and risen Christ, as communicating to the worshippers the real and true presence of the glorified Lord Jesus. Even where the consecrated bread and wine were spoken of as "symbols" or "antitypes", there was no intention to deny the reality of the spiritual presence of Christ in the holy gifts. These symbols or figures were effective signs of a reality that is actually present. The language of the early Christian writers was always strongly "realist". To sum up, the faith of the Catholic Church on this matter is that Jesus Christ is really and spiritually present in the sacrament under the signs of bread and wine.

Now some of the theological principles which follow directly and clearly from the well-known New Testament texts dealing with the Eucharist, are these. We hold that in the Holy Communion we really receive by faith through the consecrated bread and wine, the Body and Blood of Christ. He has brought the consecrated elements into a mysterious union with himself in answer to the solemn prayers of his Church and in fulfilment of his own promise. He has, as it were, taken them up into the fullness of his glorious and heavenly life, and made them the vehicle of imparting that divine life to his members, that is to the living members of his own Body. Thus Jesus Christ is, in a real and spiritual sense, present not only in the faithful and devout communicants, but also in the consecrated elements. But we do not affirm anything as to the manner of this union of Christ with the bread and wine. His real presence is spiritual, not material.

The third sentence of Article 28 describes the real and spiritual presence of the Lord Jesus in the liturgical action of the Eucharist, and especially during the act of communion, in these words:

> The Body of Christ is given, taken, and eaten, in the Supper, only after an heavenly and spiritual manner. And the mean whereby the Body of Christ is received and eaten in the Supper is Faith.

In this sacrament, Christ himself meets his brothers, all those Christians who come to him in faith and with love. He gives them communion in his death and resurrection, making them partakers of his risen and glorious life. But this is not an individual encounter between the believer and his Lord; Christ's people are nourished with his life because they are members of his body, so that at every Eucharist the whole Church is renewed and, as it were, reconstituted as the Body. Jesus Christ himself is present in this sacrament of love, he is known by his faithful, his life is received and shared by faith, by a loving faith. It is through this faith, the loving response of personal trust and self-commitment, that his people, the believers, feed on the Bread of Life, on his Flesh given for the life of the world, and taste of the fountain of immortal life.

All these statements have been clearly deduced from the New Testament texts on the nature of the Eucharist, and are therefore theological principles. But, when we come to the theological (and therefore rational) systems, speculations, and opinions as to the manner of Christ's presence in the sacrament, we enter the sphere of attempts to "understand" the mystery by the use of human intelligence. Many differing theological traditions have developed as to the way in which this sacramental presence is to be conceived, but this problem is of little importance in comparison with the fact—which is recognized by all theologians—of Christ's real and spiritual presence, or even with the experience of Christians that in the sacrament each one indeed meets personally his Lord.

From the fourth century onwards theological terminology on the subject of the conversion or the transformation (the *metabolē*) of the elements became widespread. Before and after the fourth century, some theologians wrote as though they believed in the persistence of the bread and wine after consecration, while others wrote as though they held them to be no longer there as material things. In the latter part of the patristic period, the same lines of thought continued to be present, though without raising any controversy, but we can detect a tendency towards a division between the precursors of the doctrine of transsubstantiation and those who emphasized the continued reality of the bread and wine (as well as the presence of Christ's Body and Blood) in the consecrated elements. The Fathers who made the most important contributions to the early development of the eucharistic theology are St Cyril of Jerusalem, St Gregory of Nyssa, St John Chrysostom, St Ambrose, St Augustine, and St John of Damascus.

Here is an elementary summary of the principal theological views and systems which were advanced, taught, and hotly defended at the time of the Reformation; all of them (expect perhaps the Lutheran theory of consubstantiation) are still upheld by theologians in some Churches.

(i) The theology of the Eucharist taught by Ulrich Zwingli is purely symbolic. This theory of "bare signs" makes Christ's presence depend upon the extent to which the elements of bread and wine evoke subjectively faith and devotion in the communicating worshippers.

(ii) According to Martin Luther's theory of consubstantiation, after the consecration the substances both of the Body and Blood of Christ, and of the bread and wine co-exist with each other.

(iii) The theory of receptionism proposed by John Calvin is a kind of compromise between the Zwinglian and Lutheran theories. Calvin taught that, after the consecration, the bread and wine remain as they are, only tokens of the inward grace, but that the devout communicant does indeed by an act of faith receive the Body and Blood of Christ, at the very moment when he receives the bread and wine. This Calvinistic theory has been frequently held in the Church of England, and many loyal members of this Church, especially of the Evangelical tradition, still hold it.

(iv) The medieval Roman Catholic doctrine of transubstantiation was rejected and condemned by all the Reformers of the sixteenth century.

At that time, transubstantiation had already been defined (at the Lateran Council of 1215) as a dogma *de fide* by the Western Church. It was a specifically theological attempt to define in philosophical terms the relation between the divine gift of Christ's presence and the elements of bread and wine. Transubstantiation was therefore the conversion of the whole substance of the bread and wine into the whole substance of the Body and Blood of Christ, only the accidents (i.e., the appearances of the bread and wine) remaining. The word "transubstantiation" was in widespread use in the later part of the twelfth century, but the theological elaboration of this theory was not completed till after the acceptance of Aristotelian metaphysics later in the thirteenth century, when it found its classical formulation in the teaching of St Thomas Aquinas. It was reaffirmed as a dogma *de fide* at the Council of Trent in 1551, and it is still an article of faith in the Roman Catholic Church. It has been strongly—and unhappily—reaffirmed as such by Pope Paul VI in his Encyclical *Mysterium fidei* (1965).

This doctrine is clearly excluded in the Church of England by Article 28 of the Thirty-nine Articles, in these terms:

Transubstantiation (or the change of the substance of Bread and Wine) in the Supper of the Lord cannot be proved by Holy Writ; but is repugnant to the plain words of Scripture, overthroweth the nature of a Sacrament, and hath given occasion to many superstitions.

2. THE IMPOSSIBLE UNITY IN THEOLOGY

In my opinion Catholicism and Protestantism considered as theological systems are quite incompatible and incapable of any theological synthesis. These schematic theological systems are very different indeed from Catholicism and Protestantism considered as living realities rooted in the Christian faith. Both of them are nourished with the one and same faith, even if it is sometimes viewed in a somewhat unbalanced manner. Both of them are helped, comforted, and uplifted by the same grace of the same Lord Jesus, present and active in the power of the Holy Spirit. It is this reconciling grace which is at work within all the faithful which creates the one universal Christian style of prayer, life, and action, which makes it increasingly easy for all to use the same prayers and hymns, and to read the same theological, exegetical, and devotional books.

In our ecumenical era we need, in all our still separated Churches, to build together an increasing body of agreed theological principles or fundamental doctrines, by a common effort of mutual understanding, as the result of a dialectical and serene debate. We, theologians of the still separated Churches, need to create, in this sense, a positive and constructive ecumenical theology, at the level of general principles, which can do justice to all the common theological views on which, in spite of the diversity of their terminology and of their traditional systems, Catholics (including of course Orthodox) and Protestants are coming to agree.

But let us consider briefly what are the characteristic features of the two theological systems as systems, the Catholic (especially the Roman

Catholic) and the Protestant. In the form in which each took shape in the second half of the sixteenth century, they became two powerful blocks or systematic units. In each block there was an inextricable mixture and confusion of Catholic faith, theological principles, theological opinions, theories, and rational systematizations. The truth is that at that time the Reformers, including the English Reformers, parted company with the Roman Church, and especially with the papacy, because they saw clearly and in the honesty of their consciences that their theological views, opinions, and theories could not be reconciled with those of the Roman and "Popish" theologians. Of course, as systems or as parts of a system, this was true, and still is true.

Catholicism (which includes not only Roman Catholicism but also Orthodox and Anglican Catholicism) considered as a logical and theological whole, and Protestantism (including the Anglican Conservative Evangelicals) considered in the same way, are two theological systems built on different axioms or main presuppositions. Doctrines, opinions, and observances which are common to both, may be seen by each in a different perspective, and have a different meaning to each. What then are the axioms or presuppositions underlying the two big systems, if they are subjected to schematic analysis?

The presupposition of the Catholic system is that of fullness or wholeness. If there is a sense in which wholeness or comprehensiveness is an Anglican ideal, there is a much deeper and truer sense in which it is at the heart of Catholicism, not only of the Roman Catholicism. The true Catholic or Orthodox faith is the faith which embraces the whole revelation of God for all sorts and conditions of men; and the true Catholic Church is the Church which is the right one for all men, everywhere and always. Catholicity means holding to the fullness of the Catholic or Orthodox faith, and heresy is the substitution of partial and one-sided dogmatic and theological views or speculations for the whole of the Catholic faith. This is the axiom or main presupposition, to which the Roman Catholic Church has consistently appealed in her wiser moments, for instance in the Constitutions, Decrees, Declarations, and Messages of the Second Vatican Council (1962-5).

In the past many theologians of the Church of England and of the Orthodox Church who argued that Roman Catholicism was not true and full Catholicism, did so by turning this Roman Catholic axiom of fullness against the Roman Catholic Church herself. They argued that she professed to have the wholeness of the Catholic faith, but in fact

103

fell short of this fullness, especially by the compulsory addition of the Marian and papal dogmas to the whole of the Catholic faith.[1]

A different axiom or main presupposition lies at the heart of Protestantism considered as a system. It is not just by chance that the Protestant movement of the sixteenth century appeared in history as a "Reformation", for the idea of purity, with its accompanying fear of corruption, dominates Protestant systematic theology, in the same way that the idea of fullness or wholeness, with its accompanying fear of sectionalism and schism, dominates the Catholic systematic theology, and not only the Roman Catholic theology. This Protestant idea of purity is in itself a useful, necessary, and noble conception. It plays a great part in the Catholic ideal of perfection also, especially in the discipline of the spiritual life and of monasticism, both in the East and West. But purity is not the overriding axiom of the whole Catholic system; in contrast, Protestantism made it the ruling criterion and the results were revolutionary.

The theological axiom underlying Protestantism at its best may also be described as a vivid and demanding sense of priorities. As such it should be a corrective criterion, very necessary indeed, but never a constituent factor. The real core of what is *positive* in Protestant thought and life is not its well-known and loud protest against this or that Roman Catholic or Orthodox error, deviation, or abuse. It is rather its impassioned insistence on the freedom and sovereignty of God's grace freely given to all, on the centrality of Christ, and on the conviction that everything has to be seen and appreciated in relation to God's reconciling grace in Christ.

But, behind this conflict between two main theological presuppositions, we can detect something deeper and still more intractable, a conflict of mentality and outlook, a conflict, often unconscious, of temperamental attitudes and intellectual reactions against the doctrines, traditions, and practices of the "others".

The Catholic axiom of fullness or wholeness is the expression of an attitude of obedient docility, in the best sense of these words, springing from the belief that the community of Christ's people bound together in the bond of love is really guided by the Spirit of truth to apprehend and teach the truth. But the danger is, of course, of an inert and uncritical adherence to habit, custom, and authority, and especially in the Roman Catholic Church, to the teaching authority, to the "Living Voice" of the *Magisterium*.

On the other hand, the Protestant axiom or criterion of purity, or of the sense of doctrinal priorities, expresses a questioning attitude, a disposition to sift and judge, a readiness to hold aloof, or even to reject. At its best, it is manifested as a spirit of critical caution, of wise suspension of judgement and creative scepticism; but, when it is given unimpeded sway in the mind, it sets up a fixed habit of suspicion and incredulity. Thus it can become a threat to the integrity of the Christian faith, whose purity it professes to defend.

It is only if we take into consideration this conflict of temperament, mentality, and outlook that we can understand the partly ambiguous and the partly erroneous character of Protestantism, especially in the last two centuries. Many of the central affirmations of the Christian faith are indeed present in it, and are firmly kept and proclaimed. But, side by side with them, we also find that spirit of suspicion and denial which determines the Protestant attitude of opposition to so many things in Catholic (Roman Catholic and Orthodox) thought, discipline, and life. Even the affirmations of the Christian faith are themselves made into denials; they are flung out as protests and manifestos against something or someone. Unhappily this spirit of negation is very near to the centre of the Protestant theological *system*. Therefore we cannot be surprised to find out that the Protestant mentality gave birth to rationalism and to theological anti-dogmatic liberalism, finally to secular humanism and to the theology of "the death of God".

Of course, to say that the Protestant system is infected with error is not to say that pre-Reformation Western Catholicism was free from it. It was not; nor is post-Reformation or post-Tridentine Catholicism yet free from it, even now in this ecumenical and post-conciliar (Vatican II) era. Rich in her treasures of Christian faith and life, adorned with the genuine holiness of many of her children, and strong in her historical continuity with the past and with the undivided Church, Rome, even Rome, had and has still a spirit of error within her; and this too, in its own way, is a spirit of negation. It is seen in the fact that the fundamental relationships in this Church were conceived too exclusively as relations of authority and obedience;[2] that the understanding and interpretation of the Scripture was reserved for the clerical hierarchy; and that the See of Rome, the pinnacle of the whole hierarchical and juridical structure, could say of itself that it judges all and is judged of none. It is seen in the authoritarian tone adopted by the Popes, from the Middle Ages until the accession of the good and saintly John XXIII, and also in general by the Roman Catholic hierarchy, and in the Curial impatience of any show of legitimate independence, at least until the Second Vatican Council. The reactionary, scholastic, and anti-modern teaching of Pius XII in his famous (or notorious) Encyclical, *Humani Generis* (1950) is a painful reminder of this overbearing and oppressive tendency of the post-Tridentine papacy until John XXIII. Unhappily *Humanae Vitae* (1968), the recent encyclical on birth control of the present Pope, Paul VI, showed the same authoritarian tone.

My last remark is about the mystical and "apophatic" theology of the Eastern Church. It is very important to point out the fundamental difference of mental attitude between the great theological systems of the Eastern Church (apophatic theology), and of the Western Churches (cataphatic theology), in regard to the degree of confidence which is granted to the discursive and technical use of human reason.[3] These different and fundamental theological attitudes, these different mentalities concerning divine realities, may explain, at least in part, the prolonged and constant mutual lack of comprehension between the Christian theologians and theologies of East and West. They may also explain the rather unhappy and controversial nature of the *dialogue de sourds* which has continued between East and West until the present century.

In this section I tried to make clear that Catholicism and Protestantism, considered as theological systems, are quite incompatible. All the theological systems which have been constructed by Roman Catholic, Orthodox, Anglican, Lutheran, and Calvinist theologians, are, as systems, wholly incompatible, because they are different and conflicting human systems.

3. THE ONLY POSSIBLE UNITY IN THEOLOGY

No one system, not even one as powerful and majestic as Thomism, can therefore be imposed on every mind as *the* perfect and final Christian theology suitable for all men and all times. But the Catholic axiom of fullness or wholeness, and the Protestant axiom of purity or of a vivid sense of priorities, must both find their place in a healthy and balanced Christianity, especially in any new Anglican and Catholic synthesis which should be based on the recognition of some fundamental theological principles firmly established on the Catholic faith. This theological synthesis would include what is true, positive, and valuable in Roman Catholicism and in Protestantism. It would include also the other theological and spiritual elements which are still kept alive in the Orthodox Church, but which the Western Churches have almost completely forgotten or neglected.

I. A DIALECTICAL DEBATE IN A DIALECTICAL CHURCH

Because they are man-made systems, created by the use of logical thought, both the Catholic and Protestant systems are capable of serious deviations from the whole truth, even though they contain true and valuable elements. If therefore Anglican theologians are to try to reach some theological synthesis, the first problem which they must face is one of criticism. It is to discriminate, to sift, and to determine, if possible, where each system has in fact deviated and degenerated, and then to try to restore it in outline to its true and proper form. It is only when the underlying principles of Catholicism and Protestantism are each seen in their best light and fullest perspective that the crucial questions can be asked. What, in a healthy Christianity, is the right relationship between the axiom of fullness or wholeness, and the axiom of purity or the acute sense of priorities? What is the best relationship between the two attitudes which underlies these axioms? What is primary, and what is secondary?[4]

When the Catholics and the Protestants of the West come to establishing their common theological principles and defining their relative positions, they will certainly consider the third great presentation of the Christian faith as a fixed point from which they can take their bearings, the faith of the Orthodox Churches of the East.

Before, during, and since the Reformation, the apostolic faith has lived on in the Eastern Orthodox Church, substantially unaffected either by papal or Protestant innovations and deviations, as, in fact, an example of non-papal Catholicism. This Church presents us with the faith and life of the ancient and undivided Church of the first millenium, not as a historical memory but as a present fact. I am not now thinking of the actual situation in which the contemporary Orthodox Church is placed, for every Christian Church, whether of the East or West, exists in this world in an ambiguous situation, partly living up to its faith and partly betraying it. But I am speaking here of the Orthodox faith, and not of Orthodox *theologoumena*, theology, or theological systematization. I claim, with Professor H. A. Hodges,[5] that the Orthodox faith—the faith to which the Orthodox Fathers, and especially the Greek Fathers, bear witness, and of which the Orthodox Church is the abiding keeper—is the Christian faith in its true and essential form to which we all aspire and by which we are all judged. The wind of the Spirit, bringing the gifts of wisdom and understanding, blows where it will, both in the East and West.

We Western Christians can use the Orthodox faith as a stable position from which to take our bearings. With this faith (as distinct from Orthodox *theologoumena*,[6] and from the theories and systems of any particular Orthodox theologians) in our minds, we can analyse the conflicting post-Reformation theological systems of the West, in all of which truth is mingled with error, though not everywhere to the same extent. We can then set aside and reject what we find to be false or unbalanced or one-sided in each Western system. Then, after this critical sifting, we may keep all that is true and valuable, and place in its proper setting all that we find to be balanced and healthy. The setting will be that of a lively and rediscovered Orthodoxy, or rather an Orthodox faith, for the spiritual benefit of all Western Christians.

If this is an accurate assessment of what needs to be done, then I believe that the theologians of the Anglican Communion are probably in a better position to do it than any other Christians of the West. But their task will be a more painful and demanding one than is suggested by the easy and conventional phrases which we at times hear about "the Anglican synthesis between Catholicism and Protestantism". The real Anglican synthesis will be difficult to find and will be reached only after a struggle; it will be a synthesis in matters of faith *and* of theological principles. The true Anglican synthesis is not, I repeat, a synthesis of Roman Catholicism and Protestantism as such, or (more precisely) of their theological systems; these are in fact incompatible. It is *the synthesis of those theological principles* which both hold in common, and which they will recognize that they hold in common. It is a synthesis of what is true in *living* Roman Catholicism and in *living* Protestantism, combined with the other elements of truth which both have almost forgotten or neglected, and which are still kept in the Orthodox Church.

It is only in a dialectical and dynamic debate that we shall be able to determine the conditions and the contents of this Anglican synthesis. But such a debate will not be held in a session in which the actual traditions and schools of thought that now exist in the Church of England will be ranged one against the other. It will not be a controversial dispute, but rather a debate in which each tradition and school will be ranged as much against itself as against the others, in a joint and charitable search for truth and especially for a body of common theological principles which transcends them all. In philosophical language this kind of multilateral debate is called "dialectical"; this Socratic or dialectical method requires mutual frankness combined with fundamental analysis and self-criticism, in the form of a constructive and rigorous dialogue.

Such a debate, conducted in depth and with mutual love, could be held in ruridecanal chapters, where the clergy of the deanery might engage in theological conversation and discuss peacefully their theological differences, bringing out and clarifying their common principles, and reducing their disagreements to a truer proportion. One can also visualize Catholic-Evangelical congresses, to carry the debate to a wider sphere, and in the same atmosphere of mutual frankness and sincere self-criticism.

Yet another forum for such a dialectical debate could be the Commission for the Study of Christian Doctrine in the Church of England which was established in March 1967 by the Archbishops of Canterbury and York. Its purpose is "to consider and advise upon doctrinal questions submitted to it from time to time by the Archbishops, and to plan, when desirable, the investigation of questions by other groups".[7] This Commission is a permanent body, of which one of the main duties will be to conduct in depth such a theological debate.

May I express the hope that the members of this Commission will discuss, constructively and with an open mind, all the burning theological problems with which the Church of England is now confronted? May I also hope that they will present to us the result of their dialectical debate in the form of a statement of commonly agreed theological principles in the Church of England?

But these debates should not be confined to learned and polite discussions between academic theologians representative of different traditions and schools of thought. This dialogue, which should include the active participation of laymen, must be continued throughout the Church, wherever this is intellectually and practically possible. All of us have to heal our present theological divisions, wherever this can be done, without disloyalty to the gospel and the Catholic faith; all of us, as members of a national Church which is also a part of the Catholic Church, must accept the spiritual obligation to live together in unity and charity. This will then bring people of the different theological traditions together and, at their meetings, they will effectively challenge, correct, and enrich one another. Only in this way will each theological tradition come to recognize what is false or distorted or one-sided in its own life and theological opinions, and what is true and good and Christian in the life and opinions of the others.

In the daily life of the Church we see different Anglican traditions drawing together. This must raise our hopes that, in practice as well as in theory, differences in theological opinions and in liturgical usages will be seen, more and more clearly, in their right proportion, and then out of the present disagreements, there may emerge a considerable body of theological principles on which the majority of theologians and of churchmen and churchwomen can agree. When we really want to learn from others, and be corrected by others, it will be possible to have a constructive discussion between the two main traditions on their common faith, on their liturgical customs and theological views. But such meetings—whether within the Church of England or in a wider field—will only be possible, if our spiritual life has reached a high level, for they will make great demands on the humility, patience, and readiness for self-sacrifice of those who take part.

If the members of the Church of England are able to join in a dialectical and multilateral theological debate, such as I have outlined, then we shall be able to describe her as the pre-eminently dialectical Church of Christendom. If she can be constantly debating her own position in this manner, and with the active participation of theologians of other Churches, especially those of the Catholic tradition, things may happen within her which will be felt far beyond her own national borders.

This may all seem like wishful thinking, in view of the present controversies, indecisions, and weaknesses of the Church of England. But her unreadiness to recognize her dialectical character may only be the result of the fact that she is still too tied to a particular nation and to a national Establishment, and that she has not recognized yet that she is, by her own nature and structure, a fully dialectical Church among the Western Churches. Up to the present time she has too often appeared to be content to let her various theological traditions coexist in a more or less tolerant and friendly manner, giving too often the impresssion of having no higher ambition than to keep a kind of precarious peace within her borders by letting sleeping dogs lie.

Every Church which truly deserves to be called "dialectical", and which accepts and welcomes that character, must adopt a somewhat unusual attitude towards herself. The Church of England, as a Church combining many traditions, cannot identify herself unreservedly with any of the contending theological theories, opinions, or systems, whether Catholic or Evangelical, Modernist or Radical (the "New Theology"). As a dialectical Church she will be the more committed to the view that these traditions and opinions must all be transcended in a higher synthesis of commonly agreed theological principles. Then, by this dynamic process of thesis, antithesis, and synthesis, she will then raise her own life to a higher pitch. Her present character must be affected by these continual dialectics, and undergo a progressive and deep change, as she moves towards a less imperfect solution by way of this dynamic and dialectical process.

II. POST-REFORMATION CONFLICT AND ECUMENICAL RAPPROCHEMENT

(1) *Two conflicting interpretations of the gospel* In order to assess the difficulties attending this dialectical debate, we must examine very briefly what was—and still is—the real root of the theological conflict between Catholics and Protestants which came to the surface at and after the Reformation. As a result of the schism which then broke the unity of the Western Church, two interpretations of the gospel and the Catholic faith were clearly formulated, based on different starting-points and methods of approach.

Since the Council of Trent, the Roman Catholic believer has approached the gospel almost exclusively through his own historical Church—for him, the Roman Catholic Church. For him, this Church was—and still is—the divine society founded on earth by Christ and united to him as her head. In her, therefore, is kept the fullness of grace and truth. She, with her unbroken history, hands down the gospel and the Catholic faith, interprets them with authority, and transmits from age to age the grace of God in her sacramental life which is guaranteed by the ordered continuity of the divinely instituted hierarchy. Salvation is attained through devout membership of the Roman Catholic Church, and is expressed in a gradual growth in holiness and so in the favour of God. This gradual process develops through the acceptance of the teaching of the Church, through the use of her means of grace, and through submission to her moral and ecclesiastical discipline. Reverence is certainly paid to the Bible, but always in a very close connection with the Tradition of the Church; the Bible is completed by this tradition and the teaching authority of the Church. The importance of the ecclesiastical authority, and especially of the papal *Magisterium,* is strongly emphasized.

On the other side, the Protestant believer (and in this term I include the Anglican Evangelical) approaches the gospel and the Christian faith almost exclusively through the Bible. For him Holy Writ is the divinely inspired record and instrument of the divine revelation which, once given in history, is therein set forth once for all time. By the power of the Holy Spirit, this Biblical revelation becomes a living contemporary Word through which God addresses each new generation Through the Bible and the sacraments of the Gospel (namely Baptism and the Lord's Supper), Christ draws near to men with his grace and love, and unites them to himself by faith. Salvation is attained through hearing, and responding to, the preached Word of God, and consists in a personal relationship to God in Christ. It is a relationship of sonship and reconciliation within which alone moral growth is possible. The historical Church is truly united to Christ through the faith of the faithful; but she is always imperfect, and must grow and correct herself by constant reference to the biblical Word of God. The Church is none the less reverenced as the guardian and keeper of Holy Writ, whose tradition is to be valued in the interpretation of the biblical truth.

It was inevitable that this clear-cut difference of approach by post-Tridentine Roman Catholic and Protestant believers to the historic revelation of the Christian Faith has affected deeply the way in which the two theological traditions have understood the divine revelation, both as a whole and in its different parts. Starting from different viewpoints, each tradition saw the various parts of the whole revelation in a different perspective, and so each received a different picture of the whole.[8]

The immediate results of the Reformation schism was that the four great traditions that then emerged—the Lutheran, the Reformed or Calvinistic, the Anglican, and the Roman Catholic—worked out their respective doctrinal positions in complete and deliberate isolation, in spite of the strenuous but unavailing attempts at co-operation and mutual understanding made by a few eirenic and ecumenically-minded theologians of all traditions. Each tradition, represented and backed by a particular Church, drew the full logical consequences of its own unduly narrow basis, entrenching itself in a firmly held theological position, so as to protect itself from the onslaughts of the others, and to be able itself to proceed to the attack. This militant isolation and merciless controversy of the past has left its monuments in the form of long, intricate and authoritative "definitions of Faith" and condemnations of heresies, such as the dogmatic Decrees of the Council of Trent (1545-63) and the Westminster Confession of Faith (1648), with its wide exposition of Presbyterian or Calvinistic theology.

(2) *Pietism and Rationalism*   But, however much each separated Church of the West wished to remain mutually hostile and to live in a water-tight compartment, the post-Reformation Churches could not remain for ever static, and the conflict between the different traditions has been seriously affected by at least three factors. These are, first, the influence on both Roman Catholic and Protestant traditions of various

movements of thought, notably Pietism and Rationalism; secondly, the change of spirit which has resulted in a new sense of fellowship in Christ and in a new desire to learn from one another, of which the Ecumenical Movement is the most significant illustration; and finally, the experiment which we see in the Anglican Church of today of combining elements of both traditions in the one Church.

We shall not dwell at length on the two movements of Pietism and Rationalism, because they are outside the scope of this book. About Pietism one may note that in England it affected the founders and the people of the Methodist and Evangelical revivals. In English Protestantism this renewed emphasis on the experimental element in salvation resulted in a quickening and deepening of spiritual life, in a recovery of moral earnestness, in a new missionary zeal, and in an active concern for the application of the gospel to contemporary burning social issues.

On the other hand, and in a sharp contrast to Pietism, Rationalism is marked by that type of mind which asserts that ultimate truth can be attained in every domain by reason alone, that reason is all-sufficient for this purpose and must be free from any control. Because the rationalists completely repudiate any form of supernatural religion, they have been consistently in opposition to the Roman Catholic and to the Protestant Churches alike.

After the pervasive influence of the Enlightenment of the eighteenth century came, in the nineteenth century, the most formidable rationalist attack with the rise of natural science and of biblical criticism. For some time, the divided Churches were unable to make a full integration of the traditional Christian faith and of the new scientific and critical knowledge. For instance, the Protestant Fundamentalist theologians ignored (or seemed to ignore) all modern scientific and historical research, and reasserted the verbal inerrancy of the Bible; many Roman Catholic theologians of the nineteenth century were also professing a kind of diluted fundamentalism.

On the other side, Modernism tried to do justice to modern knowledge by rejecting or explaining away those elements which, in the accepted tradition of Christian orthodoxy, appeared to conflict with contemporary science. But in actual fact it tended to whittle away the Christian revelation itself in a mistaken attempt to accommodate it to the "modern mind". This movement gained some hold in the Roman Catholic Church, as well as in the Protestant Churches and in the Anglican Communion, though in different ways.[9]

During the first half of this century the theologians of the Roman Catholic Church were hindered by the consequences of the Modernist

movement in their own Church. They did not receive any encourage-
ment from their ecclesiastical authorities; the papal Encyclical, *Humani
Generis,* of Pius XII (1950) is an example of this official disapproval.
But even then an influential body of theologians, unseen and almost
unheard, was laying the foundations of an unbelievable theological
revolution in the sense of a genuine Christian "openness". Their work
first became apparent in the dogmatic and pastoral Constitutions, Decrees, and Declarations of the Second Vatican Council (1962-5).

(3) *Practical Co-operation and the Ecumenical Movement*   Of recent
years, there has been a new spirit at work, a new spirit in all the
Churches of active fellowship in Christ and of charitable understanding
which is having a greater influence than pietism and rationalism. Both
the Protestant and the Catholic traditions are feeling its effects, and it
shows itself strikingly in the Ecumenical Movement of this century.

The basis of this new attitude is that the two principal traditions
recognize that which they have in common is of greater value than
that which divides them; that all—Roman Catholics, Orthodox,
Anglicans, and Protestants—enjoy in their common faith a deep unity
in Christ, and that this unity goes deeper than all their theological
divisions and disagreements. From this has arisen not only a very
valuable practical co-operation in many different fields throughout the
world, putting into effect the "Life and Work" motto, but also a
notable *rapprochement* in dogma and theology in accordance with the
ideal of "Faith and Order".

Already many misunderstandings of the theological positions of the
other side have disappeared, especially in the prickly problems that
were so hotly argued, attacked, and defended during the upheaval of
the Reformation. There is now a growing tendency to get away from
the exaggerated emphasis on radical diversity and mutual exclusion
which has been developed in both the Catholic (including the Orthodox
Church) and the Protestant traditions, through their deliberate isolation
and hostile rivalry. All those Churches which are now members of the
World Council of Churches are at long last on speaking terms; their
dialectical debate on the theological issues that divide them is proving
more and more useful and creative. These Churches (that is the
Protestant, the Anglican, and the Orthodox) have not yet been able to
resolve all their theological differences, but they are learning to see
more clearly, and to define more accurately, what are the real tensions
and disagreements, so as to avoid extending these matters unneces-
sarily. They are learning to look at them in a calm and dispassionate

manner, against the background of their deeper unity in the common Christian faith.

This new attitude is not based on any vague toleration which holds that theological differences do not matter. Toleration of this kind, or doctrinal indifferentism, is without doubt disloyalty to the fullness of the truth, and is equivalent to complete scepticism. What is required in our ecumenical conversations (I do not like the word "negotiations") with theologians of our own and other Churches, is an honest attempt to combine the following two principles:

(i) Each participant (and this is true of every one, clerical and lay, and in all circumstances) must hold fast to the truth as he sees it, *unless and until* he is convinced of error. For only by holding to that personal and particular view of the truth can he hope to advance further towards the plenary theological truth.

(ii) No person, even the ablest systematic theologian, holds the fullness of faith and the fullness of the theological truth without some admixture of error, even if that error is only a matter of proportion and perspective. Therefore each must be ready to listen to the others, to learn from them, and to be corrected by them.[10]

Happily, this new attitude of mental integrity and humility is spreading throughout all the Churches belonging to the World Council of Churches, and has had a powerful influence in the gradual breaking down of the artificial walls of partition and of the hostile and jealous isolation of the two principal theological traditions. We must greet this parallel approach with the utmost joy and thankfulness.

All of us in these theological conversations address each other as living men of flesh and blood who have our own distinctive features, our own backlog of tradition, our own view-points and our own store of experiences. We view God's unique truth from different perspectives. None the less, in talking to each other and listening to each other, we are entering into a fruitful, peaceful, and Christian dialogue under the guidance of the Holy Spirit. Humanly speaking, theological truth is only to be found in the living and dialectical process of a rigorous discussion, only in the joint and humble quest for truth.

Until the opening of the Second Vatican Council in October 1962, all those theologians and lay people who hoped for the spread of this new spirit of unity through ecumenical dialogue, saw one great obstacle to their optimism: the official "splendid isolation" of the Roman Catholic Church, at least so far as her authorities were concerned. Till then, that Church remained aloof from the Ecumenical Movement, forbidding her members to take part in such reunion movements as Faith and Order (Encyclical of Pius XI, *Mortalium Animos,* January 1928), and strongly insisting on her claim to be the whole and exclusive Church of Christ.

But in the last ten years, since the death of Pius XII and the accession of John XXIII, this isolation has begun to become less rigid and, under the leadership of John XXIII and the present Pope, the Roman Church has begun to work with increasing vigour for the reunion of Christendom. All the Constitutions and Decrees of the Second Vatican Council are filled with this new spirit, and the perspective of the whole Roman Church seems to have changed. The document which shows this change of heart most explicitly is undoubtedly the Decree on Ecumenism, *Unitatis Redintegratio,* which we must recognize as the official statement of Roman Catholic policy and activity on this matter. The Decree was accepted on 21 November 1964, by all the bishops except eleven, and was immediately promulgated by Pope Paul VI. At last the Roman Church had fully involved herself in the Ecumenical Movement.

In this Decree the focus is more on a "pilgrim" Church moving towards Christ than on a movement of return of heretics and schismatics to the Roman fold. The Council has gone beyond the assertion that the Roman Catholic Church is the only true Church, and affirms that Jesus Christ in his Spirit is at work in the Churches and Communities which are outside the visible boundaries of that Church. It asserts that believers in Christ who are baptized are truly reborn and are truly brothers in Christ, and that God uses their worship to save and sanctify them.

This extraordinary and (from the Roman Catholic point of view) very generous Decree is more than the opening of a door; it breaks new ground. No official document of the Roman Church has ever before spoken of non-Roman Catholic Christians in this charitable way, and there is also a remarkable admission of guilt; the Council Fathers recognized that the divisions among the Christians are the result of sin on both sides.[11]

The results of this dramatic reversal of the traditional policy of the Roman Catholic Church towards all the other Churches, may well be epoch-making. There has always been something faintly absurd in those Protestant or Anglican projects for reunion which completely ignored the largest of the bodies of divided Christians in the world. Even now, if by chance there could be a reunion of all those Churches that are members of the World Council of Churches, it could hardly be of great significance so long as the Roman Catholic Church were outside it.

The survival of Roman Catholicism, through the crisis of the Reformation and in the modern world and its own emphatic protest against Protestant denominationalism and fragmentation, must be regarded as a great work of the Holy Spirit. When we look at the last four centuries of Christian history, we see a continuous fragmentation, a fissiparous process with which we have become so familiaar that we have come to accept it as the normal state of affairs. Throughout this period only the people of the massively Roman Catholic countries have kept alive the idea of the universal structure of Christianity and of its uninterrupted historic continuity with its past. This emphasis on a universal or supranational structure and on historic continuity represents one of the chief Roman Catholic contributions to the great ecumenical and visible Church that will emerge in the future out of the contemporary quest for reunion. Whatever other features this reunited Church may have, she will be credal, liturgical, sacramental, and visibly continuous with the whole Christian past; that is, she will be both historic and apostolic. She will be visibly and undeniably the great Catholic Church of the ages. No responsible voice in the Ecumenical Movement, and in particular no responsible Protestant theologian who is sincerely concerned with the reunion movement, would now think of denying this.[12]

4. A DIALECTICAL DEBATE ON THE CHURCH AND HER MINISTRY

To illustrate the way in which such a dialectical debate in a dialectical Church might be conducted, we can take as an example one particular —but very important—topic, the Church and her ministry. Such proceedings cannot be described in detail, but there would be three successive logical stages in the dialectical approach when applied to divers aspects of this subject. These stages are thesis, antithesis, and synthesis. By definition, the synthesis or the result of the dialectical process would be a body of theological principles including and transcending the distinct and one-sided theological emphases of the two present great Christian traditions, the Catholic and the Protestant.

A debate of this type might be held on many levels, but the two that we can here consider are, first, the one within the Anglican Church between representatives of the different traditions that exist inside the Church of England, and, secondly, the one on the highest level between representatives of all the great Churches and Communions. The object of both would be to bring out the theological principles which the participants had in common, in full agreement, or with some qualification.

In order to avoid any misunderstanding, I declare that, if in the following pages I give the official pronouncements of the Second Vatican Council as examples of a result of a dialectical debate in a dialectical Church, I do not regard these theological documents as perfect expressions of a perfectly balanced theological synthesis. I do not forget the importance and necessity of the Protestant tradition and emphasis.

I. A DIALECTICAL DEBATE ON THE NATURE OR THE MYSTERY OF THE CHURCH

The traditional Catholic emphasis on the Church as a visible and historical institution or society, bound together by visible, juridical, and institutional ties, and the Protestant emphasis on the Church as the company of believers bound together by a common relationship, inward and spiritual, to Christ her head, are the two inseparable aspects of one theological truth; they are thesis and antithesis. They supplement each other; they should be held together, and the resulting state of tension is as vital as it is beneficial; this is synthesis. Both are genuine elements of the teaching of the New Testament, and both are also part of the dogmatic Tradition of the universal Church. The New Testament teaches plainly that the Church is the spiritual fellowship of those who are in Christ; yet it assumes that this spiritual fellowship has the concrete and visible form of an institutional Church. This is particularly clear from the Pastoral Epistles.

Prior to the promulgation by Pope Paul VI, during the Second Vatican Council, of the Dogmatic Constitution on the Church, *Lumen Gentium,* in November 1964, it was widely thought that the Roman Catholic theology of the Church was marked by a heavy emphasis on her visible and institutional character; indeed the majority of Roman Catholic writers of theological treatises *de Ecclesia,* influenced by centuries of anti-Protestant polemics, have placed a one-sided emphasis on the hierarchical and juridical aspects of the Church, including the plenary supremacy of jurisdiction of the Pope *iure divino.*

The main lines of *Lumen Gentium* are pastoral, christocentric, biblical, historical, and eschatological, and its tone is strongly ecumenical.[13] Every effort was made to phrase its statements in terms which could readily be understood by other Christians and by all men of good will, and to explain the Roman Catholic teaching in a way that avoided giving unnecessary offence to persons accustomed to other modes of thought and speech. This Constitution gave us an official exposition by the Roman Catholic Church of her present understanding of her own nature without anathemas or condemnations. The two complementary aspects of the Church are clearly presented and distinguished; their interconnection is shown. The New Testament emphasis on man's personal fellowship with God and with his fellow-men (the so-called Protestant emphasis) is wonderfully explained in chapter ii, The people of God, in a phraseology that is mainly biblical.

The other New Testament emphasis on the visible life of the Church, as the essential means and the normal expression of Christian people's personal fellowship with God and with their neighbours, is treated at length in chapter iii, The hierarchical structure of the Church, with special reference to the episcopate. Of course, this long chapter presents the teaching of the Roman Catholic Church on this matter from the Roman viewpoint. The ultramontane dogmas of the First Vatican Council, dealing with the supreme and universal power of jurisdiction of the Roman Pontiff, *iure divino,* over the whole Church, and the infallibility of his teaching in certain limited circumstances, also *iure divino,* are in fact categorically reasserted and proclaimed.[14] But—and this is most important—they are put in a wider context, that of the episcopate. Even so, the teaching of some sections of this chapter is, we must admit, still plainly unacceptable to the non-Roman Churches because of its formal inclusion of the papal dogmas of 1870.

Nevertheless, this chapter is marked by a striking innovation, which appears for the first time in any official Roman Catholic statement; this is the notion of the ecclesiastical hierarchy as *collegial,* and this opens a new era in Roman Catholic conceptions of church order. Now once again, as in the patristic Church, the episcopacy under the presidency of the Bishop of Rome has a share in the leadership of the Roman Catholic Church. This is a very remarkable advance beyond the sterile extremes of traditional "ultra-montanism" on the one hand, and of traditional "conciliarism" on the other. It is no longer necessary to make a choice between the isolated supremacy of the Pope and the isolated authority of the episcopal "college". This ought to lead in the near future to important developments in the responsibilities and effectiveness of episcopal conferences of local bishops, and, above all, of the permanent Synod of bishops, without any corresponding loss of unity among the bishops, or in their communion with the head of their college, the bishop of Rome, the Pope.

I repeat that I do not suggest that the Council—even after the hard debates inside the Commission—has reached a perfect balance in the matter of ecclesiology. Far from it. But I do contend that the Council has made a very important attempt in this Constitution to assess the position of the Roman Catholic Church from her own point of view. Though still open to criticism and not in perfect balance, it is none the less a very promising draft of a higher and more harmonious synthesis between the two aspects of Christ's Church. This attempt at a synthesis is expressed in particular in chapter i of the Constitution, The mystery of the Church, which is full of biblical concepts, images, and phraseology.

This notion of the Church as "mystery" at once lifts the discussion above the level of institutional organization and administration, and establishes, as the first condition of a sound ecclesiology, the mystical and spiritual reality of the Church, her divine origin, maintenance, activity, and destiny. The Church in history is "human, all too human", made up of sinful men and women. This is true, but it is also true that her genuine spiritual dynamic force, which accounts for her continuity and her effective witness in the world, lies beyond human juridicism, manipulation, or policy. To insist on the Church as "mystery" is indeed to confess God's constant sovereignty, and the lordship of the risen and glorious Lord Jesus over his Church.

II. A DIALECTICAL DEBATE ON THE NATURE AND THE FUNCTION OF THE EPISCOPAL MINISTRY AND OFFICE

It is also necessary to emphasize (as is done unequivocally and in similar terms in *Lumen Gentium*) the aspect of the visible and social character of Christ's Church; her whole outward, institutional, and hierarchical life is intended to be the means and expression of her inward and spiritual life of fellowship and love in Christ. Therefore everything which, so long as it retains due regard for human dignity, externally binds the Church together, is a means of grace and should be thankfully received.

In particular, the continuity of her ministry down the ages and its unity transcending all the particular Churches in all the world, is most significantly expressed and made manifest by the continuity of episcopal ordination. Yet, in saying this, we are not obliged to assert that the historic episcopate in the apostolic succession, is a constitutive element of the visible and institutional Church, in the same way, and to the same degree, as are the preaching of the Word of God and the administration of the sacraments of the Gospel. We may hold the view that God, in his merciful providence and in the present conditions of many separated Churches, does still raise up and use other interim forms of ministry for the effectual preaching of his Word and administration of the Sacraments. We cannot deny recognition and honour to non-episcopal forms of the ordained ministry which, we can see, have been blessed and filled by the Holy Spirit, like our form of episcopally ordained ministry.

But we can and should state that the historic episcopal ministry, in the apostolic succession is the means by which the Catholic Church has learned, under the guidance of the Holy Spirit, to express and preserve the principle of an ordained ministry, on down the centuries and throughout all the Churches dispersed across the world. We must state that, in the great reunited Church of the future, episcopacy will truly be an indispensable part of that outward and visible unity, by which the inward and spiritual unity of Christ's people in him, will be expressed and made manifest.[15]

It is inevitable that, in a not too distant future, the theologians of the Church of England will be obliged to meet in dialectical debate and come to agreed conclusions as to the essentials of theological principles on the role and nature of the historic episcopate held by their Church. At the moment the only thing which is demanded of an Anglican is that he should recognize the fact of the historic episcopate, as a sign and token of the unity and continuity of the Church of Jesus Christ. The regime of peaceful co-existence allows Anglicans to interpret this fact with great liberty, and they may hold many different views of episcopacy, such as *ad esse, ad plene esse,* and *ad bene esse.* But this extreme liberty of interpretation is in fact safeguarded only so long as the episcopal ordination is maintained absolutely unvaried by the Church of England and the Churches in full communion with her.

Such a state of affairs is quite illogical and anomalous. A pragmatical approach to the problem of episcopate is indeed no longer sufficient in our ecumenical era. If the Church of England sincerely wishes to enter into a dialectical debate with the Methodists and the other Free Churches, and also with the Roman Catholic and the Eastern Orthodox Churches, and if the Church of England has a genuine will to be united in a corporate union with the Churches of the Catholic tradition, then, before her theologians can join in any form of useful discussion with the theologians of those other Churches, they will have to come to some agreement among themselves as to the nature of the episcopal office. Some general theological principles on this matter were laid down in the Report, *Doctrine in the Church of*

England (1938). These could help Anglican theologians of different traditions to reach some agreement in this matter.

But, while we might ask the Anglican theologians to accept a minimum statement on the meaning of the episcopate, we could not demand that they should all accept the view that the historic episcopate is *absolutely essential* and necessary to the apostolic character of the Church, or that the non-episcopal Churches are lacking in this character. A reasonable request for agreed theological principles on the episcopate, does not involve any such assertion. We must not be so narrow-minded as to think—far less to contend—that the grace of God flows into the existing divided Churches only by way of the historic episcopate. Still less can we contend that membership of an episcopally-ordered Church is a necessary condition of salvation, additional to the requirement of faith in Christ. No such views are required, or could ever be required, of any member of the Church of England.

III. A DIALECTICAL DEBATE ON THE ORDAINED MINISTRY

In a debate on the ordained ministry of the Church, the thesis would be the so-called Catholic emphasis on a separated, and even on a celibate, ordained ministry (such as we find in the Roman Catholic Church of the Latin rite), with the accompanying dangers of clericalism and anticlericalism, while the antithesis would be the so-called Protestant principle of the priesthood of all believers. The synthesis could be formulated in the following manner. The Protestant principle of the priesthood of all believers is true, in so far as it means that all have free and direct access to God and an equal responsibility of obedience to him. This Protestant principle must prevail against any theory which asserts that God is to be approached only through the clergy (clericalism), that there are higher and lower grades of human honour and prestige in the Church (in the "triumphalist perspective"), or that there is a double standard of ethics. A study of two chapters of the Dogmatic Constitution of the Second Vatican Council on the Church, *Lumen Gentium,* namely chapter iv, The Laity, and chapter v, The Call of the whole Church to Holiness, is sufficient evidence that, on this particular matter, Catholics and Orthodox should be able to agree.

Meanwhile, however, Christians of the Protestant tradition must learn to integrate their cherished axiom of the priesthood of all believers with the fact of the differentiation of functions within the

Church which is the Body of Christ; this fact has both biblical and sociological backing.

This differentiation of functions in the Church is indeed not only a matter of human convenience and abilities, but is derived from Christ, who, by his Spirit in the Church, appoints to men differing gifts and differing callings. Protestants will need to recognize that the ordained minister possesses a special charisma or divine gift which he does not share with the faithful laity. The priestly ministry of the Word and Sacraments (to use the Anglican formula) is a divine and special ordinance. Ordination as deacon and as priest is not merely the Church's authorization given to some laymen to carry out certain tasks, but the grant, by the head of the Body, the Lord of the Church, of a calling and of a special grace to perform it duly. The functions of the ordained ministry ought not to be performed by persons who have not been ordained to them.

On the other hand, Roman Catholics, Orthodox, and Anglican Catholics need to recognize more fully that the ordained ministry or the ministerial priesthood is in truth an organ of the Body of Christ, doing the work of the Body in the Body in harmony with its other members. The ordination of a deacon or a priest is not the conferment of mysterious powers on a new member of a closed group, the clergy, which can pass them on independently of the Body. Christians of the Catholic tradition should not assert that the Church depends for her very life solely on the exercise of those powers which are reserved to the clerics. Ordination of the Church's ministers (which of course includes the consecration of bishops) is the calling of God within the Body of Christ. Through episcopal ordination grace is given and authority is granted to certain persons to act as the Church's ordained ministers on behalf of the Body and inside it. In the ultimate balance the ordained ministry depends on the whole Church, rather than the whole Church on the ordained ministry. All Catholics should be able to accept these views which have the support of the Bible and of common sense.[16] The clerics or clergymen must be the servants of the Church.

Here I quote the important declaration on the common priesthood of the faithful and the ministerial priesthood which the Second Vatican Council has proclaimed in its Dogmatic Constitution on the Church:

Though they differ from one another in essence and not only in degree, the common priesthood of the faithful and the ministerial or hierarchical priesthood are nonetheless interrelated. Each of them in its own special way is a participation in the one priesthood of Christ. The ministerial priest, by the sacred power he enjoys, moulds and rules the priestly people. Acting in the person of Christ, he brings about the eucharistic Sacrifice, and offers it to God in the name of all the people. For their part, the faithful join in the offering of the Eucharist by virtue of their royal priesthood. They likewise exercise that priesthood by receiving the sacraments, by prayer and thanksgiving, by the witness of a holy life, and by self-denial and active charity.[17]

IV. A DIALECTICAL DEBATE ON THE MINISTRY OF PREACHING AND THE MINISTRY OF THE ADMINISTRATION OF THE SACRAMENTS

Another subject for a useful dialectical debate would be about the ministry of the Word and the ministry of the Sacraments. The thesis here would be the sacramental ministry which is considered, more or less rightly, as the specifically "Catholic" ministry. Some say that the Roman Catholics and the Orthodox too often regard the reading and the preaching of the Bible as merely intellectual instruction or as a spiritual exercise which prepares men for the coming of the Lord in the sacraments, but which does not actually convey Christ to them. They tend to think of the sacraments as the only means whereby the grace of God is transmitted to them.

On the other hand, the ministry of the preaching of the Word of God is considered, more or less rightly, as the distinctive Protestant ministry, and this is the antithesis. It is said of the Protestants and the Anglican Conservative Evangelicals that they too often regard the preaching of the Word as the only channel of God's grace to them and that they tend to regard the sacraments as merely seals of something already given by means of that preaching.

The full theological truth is to be expressed in the synthesis: in the Gospel Christ ordained both sacraments and preaching, and both are truly complementary, but not identical channels of the divine grace in Christ. Both are necessary.

The priestly ministry of the sacraments and the priestly ministry of the Word of God are in fact very closely linked, as the two inseparable means through which the grace of God is made available in the Church to the living faith of man; therefore no rigid differentiation between them is possible. Each of them, however, has its own distinctive emphasis, so that a full and healthy Christian life depends on holding the two of them in proper balance. Thus the preaching of the Word emphasizes the individual aspect of the Christian life, while the administration of the sacraments stresses its corporate side.

When the Word of God is truly preached, each member of the congregation is aware that God is addressing him personally; when the sacraments are duly administered, each member is aware that he is taking part in a corporate act of the whole fellowship. It would be possible to draw other distinctions between these two forms of priestly ministry, but the important matter is to realize that they are mutually necessary and complementary and cannot be separated.[18]

The Second Vatican Council made a strenuous effort to restore in the Roman Catholic Church the proper balance between the administration of the sacraments and the preaching of the Word, both of which belong to the public liturgy of the Church. Its findings on this matter are to be found in the Constitution on the Sacred Liturgy, *Sacrosanctum Concilium,* passed by an overwhelming majority of the Conciliar Fathers and promulgated by Pope Paul VI on 4 December 1963, at the end of the second session. This revolutionary document is intended to restore, reform, and promote public worship in the Roman Catholic Church. One of the most striking features of this Constitution is its emphasis on Scripture, which is said to be "of paramount importance in the celebration of the liturgy". The Constitution lays down that "there is to be more reading from Holy Scripture, and it is to be more varied and suitable", with the result that "a more representative portion of the Holy Scriptures will be read to the people over a set cycle of years".[19]

The restoration of preaching, for which the Council calls, is of particular importance in connection with the need to make the Scriptures a central feature in worship. But this real presence of Christ in sermon or homily must not be contrasted with his real presence in the Eucharist.

V. A DIALECTICAL DEBATE ON THE CORPORATE
AND PERSONAL NATURE OF SALVATION

Further progress towards agreement on theological subjects, in dialectical debate within the Anglican Church and between the Churches, must depend on an increasing appreciation by all of the vital importance of holding two sets of complementary truths, at one and the same time. During four centuries of estrangement the two different aspects of one truth have been isolated from each other, or have at least been held with a lack of the proper balance between the two complementary emphases.

It has been generally assumed that Catholic theology found its natural focus in the incarnation of the Son of God. If this is correct, then this so-called Catholic theology needs some balancing factor, if it is to be saved from the danger of minimizing the fallen nature of man and of his dependence as creature even after his redemption. Such a counterweight can be supplied by the Protestant emphasis on the atonement through the cross. Similarly Roman Catholic theology, up to the time of the Second Vatican Council, strongly emphasized the authority of the historical Roman Catholic Church in matters of teaching and government, because Christ was said to dwell in and act through her. But, since the Council, Roman Catholic theology also accepts and teaches the complementary truth which she previously neglected, that Jesus Christ, as head of the Body, is also Lord and Judge of the Church. This new theology has no difficulty in recognizing that the historical Roman Catholic Church can never again be identified simply with the whole kingdom of God.

Against this the Protestant tends to over-emphasize the fallibility of the Church, because he knows that the visible and historical Church is made up of sinful and erring men and women. In his turn, he must not neglect the complementary truth, that Christ is also immanent in her, and that her life is the "incarnational" medium through which the life and grace of Christ reach men and women.

Another instance is that the Catholic tends to emphasize the corporate nature of salvation, because he sees that Christ's will is to make and save a community, that is, the Church. The Protestant, on the other hand, tends to emphasize the personal nature of salvation; he knows that nothing less than a spontaneous and free faith and a morally responsible self-surrender to Christ based on a personal relationship, will satisfy the Lords demand.

Both these emphases on the corporate and on the personal nature of salvation form part—as thesis and antithesis—of the more complex truth, forming the higher synthesis. They do not contradict each other; they supplement and complete each other.[20]

The dialectical process towards a theological synthesis develops when the theologians of one Church, for instance the Church of England, are successfully trying to combine the complementary aspects of one and complex truth into a higher theological synthesis, by the means of a rigorous, dynamic, and continuous dialectical debate, in order that their Church may corporately hold, more firmly and deeply, the rich fullness of the theological truth.

On a higher level, the dialectical process towards a further theological synthesis develops when the representative theologians of the great Churches and Communions are successfully trying to agree to the establishment of an extensive body of general theological principles. In addition to the commonly held Catholic faith, this theological *consensus* of the uniting Churches should be the *conditio sine qua non* of the final reunion of these Churches and Communions into the great Catholic Church of the future.

7

On the way to Unity

1. ANGLICAN UNITY AND DIVERSITY

To an outsider one of the most striking features of the Church of England is the way in which she manages to combine unity with diversity and comprehensiveness in her theology, her liturgy, her social work, and her missionary activity. Many committed Christians who do not belong to this Church or to some other Anglican Church are puzzled and bewildered by this claim that the Anglican Communion is able to combine in a state of happy co-existence, and with such an extensive freedom and comprehensiveness, a unity in essentials, namely in the Catholic faith, in theological principles, and in public and sacramental worship. Yet we see that this claim is proved true by all the legitimate and healthy variants or differences which exist in Anglicanism, in its different forms of spiritual life and discipline, in the non-essential parts of the liturgy that are in use in the different Churches and Provinces of the Anglican Communion, and especially in its wide range of theological theories and elaborations of the revealed truth, all held within the compass of the Catholic faith.

The contemporary Church of England knows, of course, many difficulties and uncertainties and suffers from many shortcomings like every other Church; she is threatened from outside and from within by materialism, secularism, and even atheism. Nevertheless she continues to hold to this ideal of harmonious balance between unity and diversity. The four main "traditions" which still now make up the Anglican spectrum in the Church of England may be also seen, to a greater or lesser extent, in the other Churches of the Anglican Communion. In England and elsewhere, relations between those who belong to different theological traditions and schools of thought are happily becoming increasingly friendly, but in the present-day Church of England, as well as in the post-conciliar Roman Catholic Church, the main theological cleavage occurs in fact between Conservatives or Traditionalists, and Radicals or Progressives.

In the course of this book I have outlined the way in which the

Church of England is advancing from the former state of friendly co-existence between the old "parties" to a very promising state of practical unity, especially in matters of Catholic faith, of theological principles, and, we may add, of liturgical worship, common action, and witness. The same phenomenon of dynamic convergence towards the essentials is also manifest, to some extent, throughout the Anglican Communion.

When writing this book I have often found it difficult to decide whether the matter under consideration was one which concerns only the Church of England, or affects the entire Anglican Communion. For from the ecumenical point of view, the kind of unity which we find in the present Anglican Communion, in spite of all its oddities, shortcomings, and defects, should be regarded as an important but imperfect model for the dogmatic and theological basis of the Catholic Church that is to come.

In all the Churches of the Anglican Communion, we may acknowledge the fact that they likewise are now making some headway from friendly co-existence to a kind of practical but authentic internal unity. We saw that the Mother-Church accepts the existence of many theological "traditions" in the compass of a real unity of ethos and common action. So likewise the different Provinces of the Anglican Communion, which show such a variety of races and cultures, of politics, economics, and languages, are united by a common spirit or ethos, based on their common worship and their common consciousness of their catholicity and continuity with the early and medieval Church. The bond which unites them is another example of the "Anglican compromise"; it is a pragmatic unity in which a genuine sense of authority is combined with the full right of each constituent part to healthy spiritual freedom.

What I have called "the Anglican synthesis" is not the peculiar privilege or monopoly of the Church of England. This combination of the urge for unity and of legitimate diversity is an ideal to be found not only in the Church of England but in every Church that makes up the Anglican Communion and in that Communion as a whole. Every constituent Church that is in communion with the See of Canterbury, must develop, each in her own particular conditions, a stronger sense and conviction of her individual unity, and then of the internal unity of the entire Anglican Communion. This sense of unity and union must be based on the Catholic faith; nobody can indeed discover another "Christian faith" for himself, for the Christian faith is the Catholic faith. This Catholic faith is not only of course

129

the essential basis of the Church of England and of the Anglican Communion, but it will be likewise the unshakeable foundation of the great reunited Catholic Church of the future.

As I have said, the Trinitarian and christological faith of the Church is primarily expressed in the so-called Apostles' and Nicene Creeds, and secondarily in the Athanasian Creed. On the other hand, the christological faith of the Church is enshrined in the dogmatic definition of the Council of Chalcedon. But to have a full exposition of the Catholic faith, we must add six further dogmatic truths to the three creeds and the definition of Chalcedon. This additional dogmatic basis is, of course, fully and genuinely Catholic, even though some of the truths therein contained were first very strongly emphasized by the Protestant Reformers. These truths will have to be recognized as the additional dogmatic basis of the reunited Catholic Church. I have arranged them in pairs, and they are: (i) Justification by faith alone, and the sacraments; (ii) the Bible as holy Scripture, and the doctrinal Tradition of the Church; and (iii) the spiritual and the institutional nature of Christ's Church.

In my own mind the core of this book has been to consider the paramount importance of the Catholic faith and of the theological principles in the perspective not only of the unity af the Anglican Communion, but also of the great reunited Catholic Church of the future. My vital theme has been that the final Church unity should be furthered by the mutual search made by the uniting Churches and Communions for the theological principles which they can all accept and agree upon.

This mutual search will be made easier by two means. The first one will be the systematic application of the fundamental, but not always recognized, distinction between theological principles and theological opinions, theories, and systems. I repeat that this second distinction (the first one being the distinction between faith and theology) is quite essential and very effective in destroying many false problems and in enlarging a common *consensus.*

The second means to arrive at this agreement in theological principles is to adopt in every theological conversation the method of the dialectical debate. By this I mean a deep, rigorous, logical, and charitable dialogue by representative theologians of the Churches. This dialectical debate should take place at three distinct levels. The lowest one will be held within the Church of England herself, between appointed theologians of her different traditions and contemporary tendencies. When this Church will have reached such an agreement within herself about her common theological principles, it should not be difficult to reach a similar, or a wider, agreement between representative theologians of the Churches and Provinces of the Anglican Communion. From an Anglican perspective, this pan-Anglican level may be called the middle one of the dialectical debate. The third, and highest, level of this debate will be between duly representative theologians of the uniting Churches and Communions, including necessarily the Roman Catholic Church.

Now I wish to add a remark about the present Church of England. Almost all the leaders and theologians of this Church recognize that they must put their own house in order, before they can begin any *constructive and fruitful* dogmatic and theological debate with the official representatives of the other great Churches of the Catholic and Reformed traditions. They must first arrive at a plain, unambiguous and written Confession of Catholic faith of their own Church, worded in a short document drawn up in clear, modern and biblical words. This Confession of Faith cannot be of course a simple revision of the *Thirty-nine Articles*!

Secondly they will have to express in another unambiguous statement their *consensus* about their own agreed theological principles. This second document must not be the result of a subtle and pragmatical Anglican compromise, but of a dialectical, multilateral, and rigorous debate held inside the national Church within the compass of the Catholic faith. In my view, such a theological statement put in writing is a prerequisite *conditio sine qua non* to any general agreement in matters of theology with the non-Anglican Churches and Communions, in particular with the Roman Catholic Church and the Orthodox Church.

In this context it is my opinion that, if the theological debate had been given its proper priority in the Anglican-Methodist Unity Scheme published in 1968, the whole scheme would have been assured of a greater hope of success. The important disagreements in matters of theological principles which still divide the Church of England from the Methodist Church, in particular about the meaning of Tradition, the ordained ministry, the sacraments, and especially the Eucharist, were never properly and deeply discussed, not to say settled by the members of the Commission.[1]

2. THE MAIN OBSTACLES
ON THE WAY TO FINAL REUNION

Before we consider the main obstacles still on the way to the final reunion of the divided Churches into the great Catholic Church of the future, let us have a look at the content of the dialectical debate or theological dialogue which must be held at the highest level between representative theologians of the uniting Churches and Communions.

All these theologians, Anglican, Roman Catholic, Orthodox, Protestant of Lutheran and Calvinistic traditions, and the rest, will be faced with dogmatic and theological problems of the greatest difficulty. They will have to discuss, in logical rigour and charity and with the minimum of ingrained prejudices, such thorny questions as the sacraments in general, and the Eucharist and the other sacraments; above all, they will be concerned with the doctrine of the Church, which is the major theological problem of our time. They will also have to try to reach agreement on the nature and function of the episcopal ministry and of the papacy, on the ordained ministry and the ordination administered by bishops, on the apostolic succession, on the mutually complementary ministry of Word and Sacraments. The problem of the Anglican Orders will be discussed in due time between Anglican, Roman Catholic, and Orthodox theologians. But this problem is not now a burning one, and may be settled, after the solution of the others, in the right perspective of the priestly ministry as it is seen in the experience of the Catholic Church.

One of the main obstacles to the reunion of the now divided Churches is that none of them seems to have the genuine and active will to accept any other Church fully and whole-heartedly. Such a will involves the recognition and acceptance of the fact that the peculiar "dogmas" and church orders of other particular Churches and Christian communities can differ from one's own, and yet all be legitimate, if they are found to lie within the very wide compass of the Catholic faith. It is quite likely that the factor which keeps each Church separate from every other is not some heterodox "dogma" or unChristian church order, but the simple and obstinate refusal to accept as legitimate, that is, within the compass of the Catholic faith, some dogmatic formulation or some church order which is not precisely the same as one's own.

It is deplorable that in those spheres of activity in which a merging of forces would involve no theological problems at all (such as unified programmes of ministry to the poor at home and in the under-developed countries), the Roman Catholic, Anglican, Protestant, and Orthodox Churches still all too often operate independently. Every-where we still find this regrettable lack of mutual charity and trust. But let us hope that the present Joint Committee between the World Council of Churches and the Roman Catholic Church will develop its beneficial activities primarily (but not exclusively) in the social and economic field, especially in the help to be given to the "Third World". Many good things may come from this brotherly and charit-able co-operation.

As it is, too many Christians remain conservative, apathetic, and static; they prefer to keep their present positions, imprisoned in the ecclesiastical ghettoes of their own making, opposed to any ecumeni-cal activity, and unprepared to make any real sacrifice for church unity. When many of the political forces of the world are working towards a form of international unity which is materialistic and completely secu-larist, the Christian Churches, just because they are divided, are still hindered in their ability to help in a common social work. Yet the outward and visible sign of their vocation according to the spirit of the gospel, should be the full and happy unity of all Christian people. We must be honest and admit not only that at the moment we cannot achieve any visible, organic, and sacramental communion amongst our divided Churches, but also that this state of affairs is a grave defect in the life of the whole Church. It means, in addition, that something of the highest spiritual benefit to all mankind is agonizingly lacking. Its absence is a grievous and sinful evil; it is an actual, and to some extent a conscious, participation in the continuance of divi-sions which, made manifest in the existence of every divided Church, are an outright denial of God's saving plan for the unity of mankind through a fully united Catholic Church.

This reunited Church of the future will not be a loose federation of Churches which have come together to promote friendly mutual relations and active co-operation in social and charitable works. No, the full unity of the great Catholic Church of the future will be visible, organic, dogmatic, credal, and sacramental. According to the "Appeal to all Christian People" issued in 1920 by the Lambeth Conference, the only realistic basis for the organic and fully integrated reunion of the now divided Churches and Communions, will be Catho-lic faith and Catholic order, the Catholic sacraments, and the minis-try, recognized by all the uniting Churches, of the one holy, catholic, and apostolic Church.

8

The Vision

What of the future? It is not my intention to play the role of a prophet, still less of a soothsayer. But having considered all the data of the previous chapters, it would seem appropriate, at the end of this book, to turn our eyes towards the great Catholic Church of the future to which we as Christians are called. However long and difficult may be the way to the final reunion of Christendom, the vision can provide us with a standard against which practical plans and proposals may be tested.

Not all who call themselves Christians will necessarily be part of this visible and really ecumenical Church. There are bound to be some extreme Protestant bodies and sects which will not even try to be integrated into the reunited Catholic Church, and we must not ask for the impossible. There will always be some eccentric denominations on the fringe of the orthodox, credal, sacramental, and institutional Christianity. It goes without saying that this traditional Christianity is not at all synonymous with a fossilized, reactionary, authoritarian, and "integrist" Church.

In addition, I visualize this great coming Catholic and Ecumenical Church as a supra-national religious society which will be no longer a triumphalist, clerical, and dictatorial Church. It will be a servant Church, fully independent of the national States, mainly comprising committed members and no longer a multitude of nominal members. It will be an international and truly Christian society among many other modern societies; it will be a fellowship of brothers and sisters living for God in Christ and for others in the midst of a pluralistic, materialistic, technological, and hedonistic civilization, in the midst of a post-Christian and entirely secularized way of life.

1. THE CONDITIONS AND THE NATURE OF THE RESTORED UNITY OF CHRIST'S CHURCH

The conditions and the nature of this reintegration or recomposition of the now divided Churches into the great Catholic Church of the future will be not only doctrinal, or pertaining to Catholic faith and to theological principles. They will be also sacramental and practical, showing mutual love, trust, and tolerance.

The first and most necessary condition for the restoration of organic unity among the Churches is, of course, the acceptance of the Catholic faith. By this I mean the "deposit", the content or the reality of the faith, but not the material words of any formulation or solemn declaration of it, issued in the Church's history by virtue of her teaching authority. Once again, I remind the reader of the distinction which I have so often drawn between the divine faith and any formulation of it; such historical statements are always provisional and capable of improvement. The Churches which will make up the great Catholic Church of the future, will accept whole-heartedly the real content of the full Trinitarian and christological faith, as expressed in the Catholic creeds and in the definition of the Council of Chalcedon. They will have to accept in addition and without qualification the six other dogmatic truths which I discussed in chapter 5.

The next necessary condition must be a common search, made by the great Churches and Confessions, for a large body of theological principles, through a dialectical debate, or a charitable, intellectually rigorous, and open-minded dialogue. This search and discovery appears to me to be extremely important, second only to the sincere acceptance of the Catholic faith. This collective and gradual discovery of our common heritage in faith and theological principles is happily already in progress in the conversations held in the Department of Faith and Order of the World Council of Churches, and in the theological discussions between the great Communions. I instance the present theological conversations between the Anglican Communion and the Roman Catholic Church, between the World Lutheran Federation and the Roman Catholic Church, and between the World Reformed Alliance and the Roman Catholic Church.

The visible result of this common quest will be the drawing out of two formulas of *consensus* or agreement. The first document will be a common Confession of Faith, setting out, clearly and briefly in biblical terms, the Catholic faith, and making it more explicit and more relevant to the spiritual needs of our time. This Confession should include the six additional articles of faith to which I have just referred.

The second document will be the theological basis of the final reunion of the Churches, expressing the agreed and official *consensus* of the uniting Churches and Communions on rather a large number of theological principles, which will ensure a considerable amount of theological freedom for opinions, theories, and systems. This theological formula of agreement should include, for instance, statements on the sacraments in general and the Eucharist in particular, and on the main doctrines of a Catholic ecclesiology. We already have, in the Vatican II Constitution, *Lumen Gentium,* a good draft of such a statment, though non-Roman Catholics cannot accept the teaching of the First Vatican Council on the supreme and universal jurisdiction of the Pope and on his personal infallibility. This teaching was again reasserted in the Constitution on the Church issued by this Second Vatican Council, but put in a wider perspective, that of episcopal collegiality.

A third necessary condition will be that the uniting Churches and Communions should agree whole-heartedly on sacramental life. The future reunited Church will possess and administer the same sacraments fully recognized by all, in particular Baptism and the Eucharist, which is the sacrament of brotherly love and union, and the seal of church unity. This reunited Church will also possess and administer the same sacraments of Confirmation, Penance, and Marriage, the same orders recognized by all, with the same ordained ministers, bishops, priests, and deacons. At the same time, there will be a wide variety of sacramental rites and ceremonies, of prayer books and ordinals.

It will be inevitable that there will be one centre and focus of authority in the visible organization of this Ecumenical Church; it will be primarily pastoral in its purpose and intention, but of necessity and secondarily juridical and institutional. It may be visualized as a *reformed,* synodical, and more constitutional papacy, assisted in the central government of the Church, by a permanent and efficient elected body, representing the entire college of the Catholic bishops. In addition, there will have to be some form of civil service, because, for the reunited Catholic Church made up of men and women, a competent administration is an unavoidable necessity; but this civil service or *reformed* Curia will not be allowed to become again an executive body. It should remain the administrative centre of the Catholic Church, but nothing more. I shall return to this subject later.

May I add that this coming Church must be a truly Christian and evangelical Church in which mutual love, trust, and tolerance will be effectively and sincerely practised?

2. A HEALTHY AND LEGITIMATE DIVERSITY
IN THE REUNITED CATHOLIC CHURCH

If the main characteristic of the future Catholic Church is to have a full unity in faith, in theological principles, in sacraments, in Christian life and action, this unity will be strengthened, enriched, and made manifest by a healthy and legitimate diversity, the most obvious form of which will be her comprehensiveness in theological theories, speculations, and systems. The need for this will be dictated, as is already the case, by the mystery of the Catholic faith itself, and not just by the vague demands of the religious evolution of mankind, or to suit the practical requirements of ecclesiastical organization.

We learn both from the Bible and from the early Fathers that God is not only beyond the power of understanding of our human intellect, but also beyond any words which we can find in which we try to express our tentative understanding of his perfections, energies, and operations. It would seem to follow that, even now, in each of the still divided Churches, there must be a great latitude in the words, formulas, and images suggested and used to evoke something of the fullness of the divine majesty; such latitude will be even more necessary in the future Catholic Church. The very essence of God in his Trinity is incomprehensible; it is quite impossible for us to express it with fullness and perfect accuracy in our dogmatic and theological formulations, by the use of human words and images. Even now our human expressions of the divine truth must be varied in an attempt to show all its facets; how much more will this be necessary, when the reunited Catholic Church will include, within one fold, men and women of different nations, continents, cultures, races, and languages, with different religious and psychological backgrounds. We must nevertheless recognize that the amount of variety which will be required will always be a danger to the delicate unity of such a world-wide Church; history seems to show that, if the fullness of the Catholic faith is to be brought out and communicated to every member of this great Ecumenical Church, this cannot be achieved without creating tensions and struggles.

Another form of diversity by which the life of the reunited Church of the future will be enriched, will be the variety in matters of spirituality, of the ascetic and mystical ways, through which men seek after God and try to find him in prayer, contemplation, and love. Within the compass of the one Catholic faith, every member of this future Church will be able to praise the Lord and seek him; but at the same time he will remain faithful to the spiritual traditions of his own local Church and culture according to his own abilities. In particular, Eastern Christians will continue to practise the best spiritual, ascetic, and mystical customs of their Church. Chinese and Japanese, Indians and Africans will bring into the common pool of the spiritual life of the Universal Church all the treasures of their respective traditions, purified by Christian faith and Christian love.

I do not need to expatiate upon the need for a very large variety in liturgical prayers, rites and ceremonies, Prayer Books, and Ordinals adapted to the customs and backgrounds of the different Churches, nations, and cultures. This happy variety should manifest and confirm the underlying unity of the common Catholic faith. It will be everywhere a common participation in the same sacraments, but without material uniformity. They will be administered in a variety of languages, and accompanied by different rites and ceremonies. *Let everything that hath breath praise the Lord.*

Finally, I should mention without detailed explanation one more matter in which diversity and comprehensiveness will be required. We must admit that some *general* discipline and common canon law will be sociologically necessary to maintain order and good behaviour in a planetary Church, and that there will have to be some minimum amount of administration at the centre of this big reunited Church. At the same time, this can never be allowed to become (as has happened in the past in the Roman Catholic Church) an oppressive, legalistic, and authoritarian over-centralization. Though she must have some institutional unity at her centre, the Ecumenical Church of the future will gladly recognize and ensure that all the local and national or patriarchal Churches will have the maximum amount of autonomy (please note that I do not say full independence) in administration, in all matters of church discipline, in particular canon law or traditional customs, and in individual internal organization. Such freedom will be above all necessary for the venerable Eastern Churches. If any changes have to be introduced into their liturgy, canon law, or customs, they will themselves introduce their own internal reforms, within the compass of the Catholic and Orthodox faith, and in the peaceful communion with the other sister Churches of the *Una Sancta*.

3. SPECULATIONS ABOUT THE ROLE OF THE PAPACY IN THE REUNITED CHURCH OF THE FUTURE

While taking this look at the future, I feel bound to express my personal opinion on the controversial but very important topic of the eventual role of a *reformed* papacy in the great Catholic and Ecumenical Church of the future.

The official position of the Anglican Communion concerning the present and future papacy ("its developing role") was formulated in a report presented at the last Lambeth Conference of 1968.

As a result of the emphasis placed on collegiality at the Second Vatican Council, the status of bishops in the Roman Catholic Church was in great measure enhanced, though the teaching of the First Vatican Council on the infallibility and immediate and universal jurisdiction of the Pope was unaffected. We are unable to accept this teaching as it is commonly understood today. The relationship between the Pope and the episcopal college, of which he is a member, are, however, still being clarified, and are subject to development. . . We recognize the Papacy as a historic reality whose developing rôle requires deep reflection and joint study by all concerned for the unity of the whole Body of Christ.[1]

This very cautious statement reflects the shadow that the publication of the Encyclical, *Humanae Vitae* on the opening day of the Conference, cast over its proceedings. This declaration is none the less remarkable by the careful selection of two sentences: the teaching of the First Vatican Council is rejected "as it is commonly understood today", and the words "developing role", which were purposely chosen in preference to more static terms such as "claims" or "status of the Papacy".

Now, briefly, my personal opinion or vision. In the great Catholic Church of the future, the reformed Roman papacy will be the supreme and living centre of ecclesiastical communion. Within the whole college of thousands of Catholic bishops coming from different theological and cultural backgrounds, and especially in the ecumenical councils of the great Ecumenical Church, it is obvious that there must be a presiding bishop whose office would involve a personal and deep concern for the affairs of the whole Catholic Church. It is also quite natural and most fitting that this presiding Bishop should be the occupant of the historic see of Rome. He is, and will always remain, the first bishop in Christendom and the first of the Patriarchs as the lawful successor of St Peter, the first of the Apostles.[2] In this reunited Catholic Church, the Servant of the servants of God will play effectively the positive and irreplaceable role of the supreme centre of ecclesiastical communion. He will be the focus of active reconciliation, and of strong and loving unity within the whole Christian family at long last reunited in a perfect communion.

With a considerable number of Anglicans, I would be gladly prepared to recognize the bishop of Rome, the Pope, as possessing a primacy of service, implying both a primacy of honour and of love, in the renewed, reformed, and reunited Church of the future.

The Petrine ministry is essential for securing the unity of the Catholic Church in faith and sacraments and for promoting mutual love among the sons and daughters of the gospel, because this Petrine ministry is, and will be more and more clearly, a ministry to the whole Church. The fully understood biblical notion of ministry or service goes far beyond the legal categories of the First Vatican Council. This primacy of service of the Pope in the great Catholic Church of the future is a very different thing from the legal primacy of jurisdiction. Interpreted solely in terms of ecclesiastical power and dominion, the primacy of jurisdiction would be a fundamental misunderstanding; interpreted solely in terms of the words themselves, it would leave out of account, if not contradict, the essential New Testament element, that of service. The Petrine ministry, already exercised in the post-conciliar Roman Catholic Church, and to be more and more fully exercised in the great Catholic Church of the future, will be, according to its correct and biblical description, a primacy of loving service, a pastoral primacy.

Therefore the Servant of the servants of God in this reunited Church will be a pastor according to the spirit of Jesus Christ himself. He will not be against the law, but against legalism; not against order but against immobilism; not against authority but against authoritarianism; not against unity but against uniformity; not against Christian freedom but against abuse of this freedom.

In this reunited and truly Ecumenical Church of the twenty-first century, the Pope will have abandoned all his unbiblical and almost divine titles such as *Sanctissimus Dominus, Beatissimus Pater,* His Holiness, Holy Father, Head of the Church, Vicar of Christ, Supreme Pontiff, etc. His valid titles will be: Bishop of Rome, Pope[3], Servant of the servants of God, and chief Pastor. The present Pontiff, Paul VI, has already given some signs of such evangelical humility.

Evangelical simplicity will be the main ornament of the bishops of Rome as the chief Pastor of the reunited Catholic Church. Without indulging in unrealistic and romantic poverty, the Pope will have to renounce all the imperial pomp and luxury which are still a too characteristic feature of the Vatican "Apostolic Palace". Above all, this evangelical simplicity will be shown in the clothes of the Vatican officers and "courtiers", in the abolition or radical simplification of the courtly apparatus and protocol, of the guards of honour and the Swiss

Guard. Papal Orders and Roman court titles make indeed no sense in a Church of service.

This *reformed* papacy must give genuine evidence of evangelical brotherliness. The bishops of Rome of this period will have renounced a long time ago, everything that still now savours of absolutist and authoritarian government, the imperial Byzantine-baroque style of speaking and writing official letters or encyclicals, all secret procedures so dear to the present Roman Curia, and all solitary decisions without the co-operation of the Church, that is of the bishops. The Popes of this era of the reunited Catholic Church will no longer exercise political power; they will be no longer Heads of State, even of the tiny Vatican City; they will have renounced all secular diplomacy, in particular the sending of episcopal nuncios. They will concentrate entirely on their pastoral and spiritual task.

In the exercise of the papal ministry, the principle of episcopal collegiality on which the Second Vatican Council has put such a heavy emphasis, will have been, at last, translated from texts into effective decisions and deeds. The chief Pastor of the reunited and renewed Catholic Church will be no longer an autocrat or an absolutist ruler but in all the important affairs of the supra-national Church he will not act on his own and personal authority. In all the matters relating to the Catholic faith and to the morals of the People of God, he will always seek the previous and explicit judgement of his brothers and colleagues in the episcopate, or, if it is impossible, of the permanent and truly representative synod of bishop always present in Rome according to a rota. The Pope will be *ex officio* the president or chairman of the great Ecumenical Councils, or of this small permanent synod of bishops at Rome. In this he will be tied by a majority decision, because he will be only a constitutional ruler governing the Church in a synodical or collegial manner. In this constitutional and conciliar perspective, no Pope will be allowed to write alone and to promulgate alone such documents as the recent Encyclicals, *Sacerdotalis caelibatus* (on compulsory priestly celibacy), or *Humanae Vitae* (on birth control).

When the now divided Churches have been reintegrated into the Catholic unity, the present Canon Law of the Roman Church will already have been fully and radically reformed, and the present Roman Curia likewise radically reformed and reduced to the status of a civil service.

This sweeping reform of the present Canon Law should demand a fundamental review of the nature and functions of a Canon Law for a planetary and truly Catholic Church. This radical reform of the Canon Law must also introduce many deep alterations, omissions, and concrete reforms which will be made not according to the particular and local Roman legal tradition, but according to the gospel of Jesus Christ, and also to the needs of mankind in the twenty-first century.

Another indispensable condition for the recomposition into Catholic unity of the present divided Churches will be, as I said, the effective and radical reform of the present ultra-conservative, traditionalist and reactionary Roman Curia which makes up one of the most intractable and powerful obstacles to Christian unity. The Curial power machinery must be internationalized, and that not only superficially, but fully, and reduced to the status of a central administrative body carrying out the commands and directives of the executive power, namely of the Pope *in* Synod, or of the Pope governing *with* his episcopal brothers.

In this perspective of unity with diversity in the Catholic Church of the future, the reformed papacy itself will further and secure the full autonomy of all the sister Churches comprising the Ecumenical Church, and of their pastoral ministries according to the principle of subsidiarity which was theoretically proclaimed by some recent Encyclicals.[4]) Also all the sister Churches will themselves elect their own bishops, archbishops, metropolitans, and patriarchs (in the Eastern Churches). The different national and patriarchal Churches will receive the firm guarantee that they will retain in its entirety their present autonomous and particular Church order, their discipline, their peculiar canon law, their own liturgy, their particular ethos and theological characteristics under their own Metropolitans or Patriarchs, always in the compass of the same Catholic faith and of the same theological principles, upon which all of them have previously agreed. On the other hand, all these national Churches will have previously and whole-heartedly recognized the pastoral primacy of the Petrine or papal ministry, in particular as the supreme court of appeal mediating and settling disputes between the Churches.

My last word will be about the so-called Vatican dogmas, which make up the still apparently insuperable stumbling-block. The Marian dogmas of the immaculate conception of Mary and of her bodily assumption into the heavens may be perhaps explained away as devotional theological theories which were uplifted, by explicable error, to the level of dogmas, in a particular time, by a particular Church, and under particular historical circumstances.

But another problem seems almost insoluble. It is concerning the two papal dogmas which were proclaimed as *de fide catholica* by Pius IX at the end of the First Vatican Council (1870). They are (i) the supreme and universal primacy of jurisdiction of the Roman Pontiff over every Church and every person in the Roman Catholic Church; (ii) the personal charisma of infallibility attached to the Roman Pontiff, when he speaks *ex cathedra* on matters of faith and morals. I cannot see any immediate solution of this thorny problem. All the non-Roman Catholic churches are indeed unanimous in rejecting this teaching as it is commonly understood today.

I have a deep feeling of admiration for the intellectual power and subtlety of mind of some influential Roman Catholic theologians, who do not always teach in Rome. Either they themselves or their successors may find a happy means of rendering these specifically Roman dogmas more or less palatable to the non-Roman Catholic Churches.

Also it is always possible that, in a future and totally different theological climate, the Third or Fourth Vatican Council may promulgate a theological doctrine relating to these controversial papal dogmas. This official doctrine might give an authentic and acceptable interpretation of the two dogmas defined by Pius IX and his Council. It would be an official and providential correction of the Vatican dogmas by the Roman Catholic Church herself. There are some precedents in the history of the ecumenical or general councils.

Epilogue

Look, therefore, O Lord, Holy Father, upon us, thy servants. Illumined by the grace of thy Spirit and impelled by brotherly love, we express our repentance for sins against unity. We humbly ask thy pardon and that of our brothers, and with one voice we beg thee to grant perfect unity among those who believe in thee.

We earnestly ask thee, O Lord, O thou lover of men: pour out today upon us a new and more abundant grace of thy Spirit, that we may live our lives in a way worthy of the calling by which thou hast called us; with all humility, meekness, and patience, may we support one another in love, and be attentive towards maintaining the unity of the Spirit in the bond of peace. By recognizing the signs of the time, and through unceasing self-denial, repairing the errors of the past, may we arrive, by thy grace, at the hour of perfect communion which we all desire.

(Extract from the Latin Prayer of Praise and Thanksgiving offered by Pope Paul VI in St Peter's, Rome, on Thursday, 26 October 1967, on the occasion of the visit of the Ecumenical Patriarch, Athenagoras I.)

Notes

CHAPTER 1

1. W. F. R. Browning, ed., *The Anglican Synthesis: Essays by Catholics and Evangelicals* (1964).
2. *The Lambeth Conferences (1867-1930): Reports of the 1920 and 1930 Conferences, with selected resolutions from the Conferences of 1867, 1878, 1888, and 1908* (1948). For the Lambeth Appeal, see pp. 119-24. On the Lambeth Appeal of 1920 one may read R. Lloyd, *The Church of England 1900-65* (1966), pp. 403-42.
3. *The Lambeth Conferences*, p. 119.
4. Ibid., p. 119.
5. Ibid., p. 120.
6. Ibid., p.120.
7. Ibid., p. 120.
8. Ibid., p. 121.
9. Ibid., pp. 296-7 (1888, Resolution 11).

CHAPTER 2

1. Text in H. S. Bettenson, *Documents of the Christian Church* (1956), pp. 306-7; H. Gee and W. J. Hardy, *Documents Illustrative of English Church History* (1896), p. 187.
2. D. Knowles, *The Religious Orders in England* (1959), Vol. iii, The Tudor Age.
3. Ibid., p. 465.
4. Ibid., p. 465.
5. A. G. Dickens, *The English Reformation* (1964), p. 314.
6. Ibid., p. 315.
7. Ibid., p. 319.
8. Ibid., pp. 320-1. On the Reformation in England under the reigns of Henry VIII, Edward VI, and Mary, I wish to recommend also the careful and balanced study of T. M. Parker, *The English Reformation to 1558* (1963), in the Home University Library series.
9. H. Northcott, "The Development and Deepening of the Spiritual Life", in *Northern Catholicism* (1933), pp. 309-35, edited by N. P. Williams and C. Harris. Excellent pages on Tractarian spirituality, especially on its attitude of awe before the mystery of God and the Unseen World, on its stress on the hidden life of union with God, and on the Tractarian insistence on the need for personal holiness.
10. P. F. Anson, *The Call of the Cloister* (1955; 2nd revised edn 1964); A. M. Allchin, *The Silent Rebellion: Anglican Religious Communities, 1845-1900* (1958).
11. The Church of England Liturgical Commission, Alternative Services: Second Series (1965).

12. — An Order for Holy Communion: Report to the Archbishops of Canterbury and York, April 1966 (1966).
13. Alternative Services: Second Series: An Order for Holy Communion (1967).

CHAPTER 3

1. A. R. Vidler, ed., *Soundings* (1962).
2. J. A. T. Robinson, *Honest to God* (1963).
3. J. A. T. Robinson and D. L. Edwards, edd., *The Honest to God Debate* (1963). See also J. A. T. Robinson, *Christian Morals Today* (1964); *The New Reformation?* (1965).
4. E. G. Selwyn, ed., *Essays Catholic and Critical, by members of the Anglican Communion* (1926). The 3rd revised edn (1929) has been reprinted many times.
5. See the excellent booklet, *Catholicity: a Study in the Conflict of Christian Traditions in the West: a Report by a group of Catholic Anglicans* (1947), especially pp. 44-7 and 49-55.
6. The views of these radical and young Catholic Anglicans are forcefully expressed in the recent collective work edited by John Wilkinson, entitled *Catholic Anglicans Today* (1968). Here we find new positions, new thinking, even a new vocabulary.
7. This extremely conservative and rather shocking view of the verbal inspiration of holy Scripture and of its literal inerrancy and infallibility is, for instance, expressed with vigour by R. T. Beckwith, librarian of Latimer House, in his essay, "The Inspiration of Holy Scripture", in Browning, op. cit., pp. 27-48. See especially pp. 32-7.
8. See the characteristic essay of J. I. Packer, "The Status of the Articles", in *The Articles of the Church of England* (1964). The last words of this learned but controversial essay are: "Nothing better could be wished for the future of Anglicanism and the well-being of the Anglican Churches that the Articles should regain among us the status which is theirs by theological right" (p. 56).
9. Concerning this essential doctrine of the justification of the sinner by faith alone, and the Conservative Evangelical interpretation of this Pauline doctrine through the phraseology of the English Reformers, see the small but substantial booklet by T. C. Hammond, *What is an Evangelical?* (1960), pp. 6-13, "What Evangelicals believe". Note especially pp. 7-9. Concerning the other special emphases of the Conservative Evangelical theology, I refer the reader to this book also.
10. John King, editor of *The Church of England Newspaper*, 1960-8, has had published in 1969 a controversial, humorous, and well-documented paperback on the Conservative Evangelicals, entitled *The Evangelicals*.
11. *The Fulness of Christ: the Church's Growth into Catholicity: a Report presented to the Archbishop of Canterbury* (1950).
12. For a very pungent and forceful exposition of the authority of the Bible from the Liberal Evangelical point of view, see R. P. C. Hanson, "The Authority of the Bible", in Browning, op. cit., pp. 17-26.
13. V. F. Storr, *Spiritual Liberty* (1934), especially pp. 118-24, gives a good summary of the Liberal Evangelical position.
14. See Guy Mayfield, *Like Nothing on Earth* (1965), pp. 175-9.
15. H. D. A. Major, *English Modernism: its Origin, Methods, Aims* (1927). For the history of English Modernism, see R. Lloyd, op. cit., pp. 112-5, 258-71.
16. Ibid., pp. 98-9.

CHAPTER 4

1. *Catholicity* (1947), pp. 52-3.

Notes

2. S. C. Neill, *Anglicanism* (1958), pp. 323-57.
3. Confirmation administered by a bishop, or rather belief in its spiritual utility, coupled with belief in the paramount value of the threefold ordained ministry, is one of the powerful factors which unite everywhere ordained Anglican ministers as brothers. It is much more than a disciplinary and administrative measure.
4. Even the Tudor monarchs, in their search to establish by law a national Church, which should be clearly distinct and separate from the Roman Church, have emphasized the historical and dogmatic continuity of the recently reformed Church of England with the medieval English Church, with her bishops and her saints (especially with those who lived before the Norman conquest), and with the Catholic Church of the first centuries and her pious and orthodox bishops, saints, and doctors, both of East and West. This emphasis on the historical, dogmatic, and liturgical continuity of the Reformed Church of England with her medieval past and with the early Catholic Church, seems to be a very special feature of the Church of England amongst the other Reformation Churches. This emphasis is certainly not a particularly High Church tradition; it is an Anglican tradition which could be traced from King Henry VIII to the present Archbishop of Canterbury. The claim that Anglican Orders are truly Catholic and fully integrated within the Catholic church order is only a corollary of the general claim of the Church of England to true Catholic status and continuity.
5. See, for instance, the English translation of the Decree on Ecumenism in the useful collection edited by W. M. Abbott, s.j., *The Documents of Vatican II* (1966), p. 356.
6. In the Roman Catholic Church the sacrament of Confirmation is normally given after First Communion and one or two years before the so-called Solemn Communion.
7. W. Temple, *Essays in Christian Politics* (1927), pp. 201-2.
8. See *The Fulness of Christ*, pp. 37-56 and especially pp. 51-6.

CHAPTER 5

1. E.g., H. Küng, *Structures of the Church* (E.T., 1965), pp. 181-4, 344-51 (faith and formulation of faith; dogmas and improvement of dogmas) and K. Rahner, *Theological Investigations*, Vol. v (E.T., 1966).
2. E.g., H. A. Hodges, *Anglicanism and Orthodoxy* (1957), pp. 33-5.
3. The history and meaning of the main Christian creeds is very competently expounded in the book of J. N. D. Kelly, *Early Christian Creeds* (2nd edn, 1960).
4. Ibid., pp. 1-6 (the ancient legend).
5. For the Latin text (according to Rufinus) and the Greek text see H. Denzinger and K. Rahner, *Enchiridion symbolorum* (Munich 1957), no. 2, p. 2. For the Latin text with E.T., see Kelly, op. cit., p. 102.
6. For the Latin text of the last form of the Apostles' Creed (*textus receptus occidentalis*) see Denzinger and Rahner, op. cit., no. 6, p. 6 and Kelly, op. cit., p. 369. On the Apostles' Creed, see Kelly, op. cit., pp. 368-97.
7. For a discussion of the precise meaning of the two articles of the Apostles' Creed peculiar to the West, the descent into hell and the communion of saints, see Kelly, op. cit., pp. 368-97.
8. For the original Greek text of the Creed of Nicaea, with Latin translation by St Hilary of Poitiers, see Denzinger and Rahner, op. cit., no. 54, pp. 29-30. For the Greek text with E.T., see Kelly, op. cit., pp. 215-6.
9. Concerning the Creed of Nicaea and its meaning, see Kelly, op. cit., pp. 205-62.

10. Kelly, op. cit., pp. 296-331.
11. Ibid., pp. 235-6. See also the excellent study of A. M. Ritter, *Das Konzil von Konstantinopel und sein Symbol* (Göttingen 1965). The author convincingly contends that this Council promulgated the Constantinopolitan Creed.
12. For the original Greek text of the Constantinopolitan Creed, with Latin translation by Dionysius Exiguus and with the Latin liturgical text, see Denzinger and Rahner, op. cit., no. 86, pp. 41-2. For the Greek text with E.T., see Kelly, op. cit., pp. 297-8.
13. About this fateful interpolation of the *Filioque* in the Latin text of the Constantinopolitan Creed, see Kelly, op. cit., pp. 358-67.
14. J. N. D. Kelly, *The Athanasian Creed* (1964), pp. 35-41, 109-27.
15. Ibid., p. 23.
16. C. H. Turner, "A Critical Text of the Quicunque Vult", in *JTS* xi (1910), pp. 401-11.
17. J. N. D. Kelly, *The Athanasian Creed*, pp. 17-20.
18. Concerning the doctrine of the double eternal procession of the Holy Spirit in St Hilary of Poitiers, Marius Victorinus, St Ambrose, and St Augustine, see Kelly, op. cit., pp. 86-90.
19. For the original Greek text, with Latin translation by Rusticus, see Denzinger and Rahner, op. cit., no. 148, pp. 70-1. An accurate English translation is to be found in J. N. D. Kelly, *Early Christian Doctrines* (1958), pp. 339-40.
20. J. Stevenson, *Creeds, Councils, and Controversies* (1966), p. 337.
21. *The Fulness of Christ*, pp. 78-84.
22. See ibid., pp. 17-24 for a good survey of the Reformation doctrine of justification.
23. See *Doctrine in the Church of England* (1938), pp. 127-30.
24. E. Amand de Mendieta, *Rome and Canterbury: a Biblical and Free Catholicism* (1962), pp. 127-49.
25. Dogmatic Constitution on Divine Revelation, ch. 6. 1, in Abbott, op. cit., p. 125.
26. See *The Fulness of Christ*, pp. 61-2.
27. See ibid., pp. 64-5.
28. Dogmatic Constitution on the Church, *Lumen Gentium*, ch. 1. 8, in Abbot, op. cit., pp. 22-3.
29. E.g., ibid., ch. i. 7, in Abbott, op. cit., pp. 20-1.
30. On the Church's ministry, the historic episcopate, and the honour due to the non-episcopal ministries, see *The Fulness of Christ*, pp. 81-4.
31. On the ultramontane dogmas of the First Vatican Council, one may see my book *Rome and Canterbury*, pp. 150-78.
32. Decree on Ecumenism, *Unitatis Redintegratio*, ch. ii. 11, in Abbott, op. cit., p. 354.

CHAPTER 6

1. See Hodges, op. cit., pp. 36-7.
2. Ibid., pp. 37-9.
3. See G. de Jaifve, "East and West: Two Theologies, One Faith", in E. L. B. Fry and A. H. Armstrong, edd., *Rediscovering Eastern Christendom* (1963), pp. 51-62.
4. Hodges, op. cit., p. 39.
5. Ibid., p. 47.
6. On Orthodox theology considered as a whole, see my book, *Rome and Canterbury*, pp. 114-25.
7. *Church Times*, 23 March 1967, p. 1.
8. See *The Fulness of Christ*, pp. 39-42.

9. For a good survey of Pietism and Rationalism, see *The Fulness of Christ*, pp. 43-9.
10. Ibid., pp. 49-50.
11. For E.T. of the Decree on Ecumenism, *Unitatis Redintegratio*, see Abbott, op. cit., pp. 341-66. There are many other English translations. Here note especially pp. 341-4.
12. See J. V. Langmead-Casserley, *The Church To-day and To-morrow* (1965), pp. 62-8.
13. For E.T. of the Dogmatic Constitution on the Church, *Lumen Gentium*, see Abbott, op. cit., pp. 14-96.
14. Ibid., pp. 42-3, 47-50.
15. *The Fulness of Christ*, pp. 65-6.
16. Ibid., pp. 66-7.
17. Abbott, op. cit., ch. ii. 10, pp. 26-7.
18. See *The Fulness of Christ*, pp. 67-9.
19. For E.T. of the Dogmatic Constitution on the Sacred Liturgy, *Sacrosanctum Concilium*, see Abbott, op. cit., pp. 139-78. Here note especially ch. i. 35, p. 149, and ch. ii. 51-2, p. 155.
20. See *The Fulness of Christ*, pp. 69-71.

CHAPTER 7

1. *Anglican-Methodist Unity: Report of the Anglican-Methodist Unity Commission*, Part 2. The Scheme (1968), pp. 10-33. See especially para. 3, Agreement in doctrine, and para. 97: "These agreements [concerning the doctrine of Holy Communion], in the judgement of the Commission, form sufficient doctrinal basis for closer relations in the sacramental life of the two Churches".

CHAPTER 8

1. *The Lambeth Conference 1968: Resolutions and Reports* (1968), p. 138.
2. After the ascension Peter immediately took the lead among the Apostles and thoroughout the period covered by the first half of the Acts of the Apostles, he appears as their head. He opened the Church to the Gentiles by admitting Cornelius, and his authority is again evident at the Apostles' Council at Jerusalem.
3. Namely Pope of Rome. In the early days of the Church this title "father" was used in the West of any bishop. In the East it was apparently confined to the bishop of Alexandria.
4. This principle of subsidiarity, which was formulated by Pope Pius XI in the Encyclical, *Quadragesimo Anno* (1931), and by Pope John XXIII in the Encyclical, *Mater et Magistra*, is at least three times quoted and approved in the official documents of the Second Vatican Council, especially in the Pastoral Constitution on the Church in the Modern World, *Gaudium et Spes*. For E.T. of this Constitution, see Abbott, op. cit., pp. 199-308. Here note specially ch. v. 86(c), p. 300. According to this important principle of social philosophy, it is unjust and a gravely harmful disturbance of right order to transfer to a greater society or body of higher rank such functions and services as can be performed by lesser bodies on a lower plane.

Index